Unlocking Afghanistan's Agricultural Export Potential A Comprehensive Analysis

Rajeev Kumar

Copyright © [2023]

Author: Rajeev Kumar

Title: Unlocking Afghanistan's Agricultural Export Potential A Comprehensive Analysis

All rights reserved. No part of this publication may be reproduced, stored in a retrieval system, or transmitted, in any form or by any means, electronic, mechanical, photocopying, recording, or otherwise, without the prior written permission of the publisher or author.

This book was printed and published by in [2023].

ISBN:

Table of content

Chapter name	Page No
1: Introduction	1
2: A Look Back at the Farming in Afghanistan	15
3: The Present Agriculture Situation in Afghanistan	22
4: Products That Could Be Exported	31
5: Problems Facing Afghan Farming	42
6: Building Up the System	50
7: Sustainability through Water Resource Management	60
8: Promotion of Agricultural Knowledge and Technology Transfer	72
9: Market Exposure Abroad	87
10: Stories of Achievement and Case Studies	110

Chapter 1:
Introduction

1.1- Briefly introduce the book's topic: Afghanistan's agricultural export potential.

A Deep Dive into Afghanistan's Agricultural Export Potential

Afghanistan, a country renowned for its beautiful scenery and diverse cultural legacy, has a troubled past fraught with war and political upheaval. Many people immediately associate it with thoughts of devastated landscapes and political instability. The agricultural industry, in particular, has enormous unrealized potential beneath the surface of these headlines. This book offers a critical examination of the paths that can bring economic recovery and prosperity to Afghanistan through the country's agricultural export potential.

Afghans have shown remarkable fortitude throughout the country's history of invasion, violence, and political turmoil. It has a long and rich history characterised by several ancient civilizations, bustling trading networks, and impressive agricultural advances. Afghanistan has been an important hub for trade, agriculture, and culture since the time of the Indus Valley civilization. In spite of the difficulties of the present day, this vibrant historical background continues to serve as a wellspring of motivation and optimism.

Afghanistan in the 21st century has numerous problems, yet its potential for agricultural expansion is enormous. The nation's topography and climate are excellent for many kinds of agriculture, which is where this potential comes from. The book's overarching goal is to help Afghanistan improve the lives of its citizens by answering the question, "How can Afghanistan unlock and realise its agricultural export potential?"

Understanding Afghanistan's potential in agricultural exports is no easy feat. Decades of conflict, poor farming practises, and an absence of essential infrastructure are just some of the challenges that travellers will face on this path. It is crucial, however, to keep in mind that these difficulties are not insurmountable. Instead, they serve as chances to learn and adapt. Fact: Wheat, barley, and maize are the backbone of Afghanistan's agricultural sector right now. Although these products are essential for food security, export potential are low because the domestic and regional markets are already saturated.

This book delves deeply into the agricultural industry of Afghanistan, analysing its current situation and illuminating the challenges and opportunities it faces. Its goal is to draw attention to the latent potential that, if developed, might help drive the United States into a new era of agricultural prosperity. Afghanistan's agricultural potential, problems, possibilities, and strategies for realising that potential will be discussed in length in the following chapters.

Agriculture has played a significant role in shaping Afghanistan's history, and this chapter will provide an outline of the country's agricultural history. It will delve into the rich agricultural history that the Afghan people carry with them in their hearts and soil.
In Chapter 2, we'll look at the current situation in Afghan farming, including an examination of the most important crops and the difficulties farmers face due to issues including a shortage of water, inadequate infrastructure, degraded soil, and a reluctance to accept new technologies. Areas for improvement and expansion will also be highlighted in this section.

In Chapter 3, we'll look into the possibility of exporting Afghan agricultural goods. Pomegranates, almonds, saffron, and other expensive spices will be the main focus. This chapter will highlight the competitive advantages and growth possibilities of these items on a global scale.

In Chapter 4, we'll talk about the problems plaguing Afghan agriculture and the solutions that will help fix them. This chapter will serve as a road plan for development across the board, from infrastructure construction to water management, agricultural training to peace and safety.

The demand for Afghan agricultural exports around the world is the focus of Chapter 5. It'll look at how Afghanistan's food options coincide with modern customer preferences for organic and exotic fare from responsible suppliers.

The potential of Afghanistan's agricultural sector, including organic farming, novel irrigation methods, and the use of cutting-edge agricultural technology, will be explored in further depth in Chapter 6. This chapter will highlight these chances as vital catalysts for development and change.

In Chapter 7, we'll look at why it's crucial to invest in transport and storage infrastructure. Current and future initiatives to strengthen the agriculture industry will be outlined.

Understanding that water is essential to agricultural production, Chapter 8 will examine sustainable water management practises. Effective water management strategies, the effects of global warming on water supplies, and long-term fixes will all be covered.

The importance of training programmes and technical improvements to increase productivity and product quality will be emphasised in Chapter 9. This chapter will focus on agricultural education and the adoption of technology.

Getting into foreign markets is a significant topic that will be discussed in Chapter 10. Promotion of Afghan goods, guaranteeing adherence to trade legislation, and negotiating trade agreements with importing countries are all covered in detail.

Finally, Chapter 11 will showcase the achievements of Afghan farmers and business owners who have tapped into the country's vast untapped potential in agricultural exports. The transforming force of agriculture and its effect on rural areas and the national economy will be shown via these narratives.

This book is an ode to the perseverance of the Afghan people and their contributions to the agriculture industry. This study aims to contribute to the national and global discourse about how agriculture may pave the road to wealth and stability in Afghanistan by exploring the difficulties, opportunities, and potential for agricultural export. Unlocking Afghanistan's agricultural export potential is a story of struggle and triumph, and a tribute to the resilience of the Afghan people.

1.2- Highlight the importance of this analysis for Afghanistan's economic development.

An In-Depth Look at Afghanistan's Agricultural Export Potential

Introduction

Afghanistan, a country known for its verdant landscapes, complex cultural fabric, and old customs, has a history of upheaval and difficulty. International media coverage of Afghanistan typically focuses on war, political unrest, and the country's never-ending fight for peace. The great potential of Afghanistan's agriculture sector to fuel economic development, however, is buried under layers of hardship and uncertainty and has not gotten its full respect.

This in-depth study was conducted with the intention of stressing the significance of recognising and capitalising on Afghanistan's agricultural export potential. This isn't just an intellectual exercise; it's an investigation of potential paths to economic growth in Afghanistan. This is a major acknowledgment of agriculture's potential to radically alter a country's economic trajectory and boost people's standard of living.

Afghanistan's Agricultural Heritage (Chapter 1)

The importance of this study can only be grasped by first learning about the origins of agriculture in Afghanistan. Ancient agricultural developments have left a lasting imprint on Afghanistan's history. As a former cultural and imperial crossroads, this area has a long history of agriculture that continues to impact its present and future.

There are two reasons why this historical context is so crucial. For one, it highlights Afghanistan's rich agricultural history. Second, it stresses the importance of building on past practises to ensure a long-lasting future.

The Present Agriculture Situation in Afghanistan (Chapter 2)

It is essential to perform a thorough evaluation of the current situation of Afghanistan's agricultural industry before digging into the potential for agricultural exports. This section aims to provide a thorough analysis of the difficulties and potential solutions facing agriculture in Afghanistan.

The chapter's analysis is helpful in demonstrating the pressing need for revolutionary change in agriculture in Afghanistan. Staple commodities like wheat, barley, and maize will show up prominently, despite their low export potential due to domestic and regional market saturation.

Chapter 3: Products That Could Be Exported

The incredible potential of Afghanistan's agricultural diversity is the focus of this chapter. It provides a comprehensive and complete analysis of the agricultural commodities, fruits, and goods that can be exported from Afghanistan. Here, we'll zero in on high-priced crops like pomegranates, almonds, saffron, and spices for their individual desirability on global markets.

The goal is to create an interesting story about these goods, stressing their significance in the development of Afghanistan's economy. In this chapter, we lay the groundwork for imagining a future in which Afghan agricultural exports are well-known and in demand around the world.

Issues Facing Afghan Farming (Chapter 4)

A thorough understanding of the significant issues facing Afghanistan's agricultural industry is necessary to realise the significance of addressing the agricultural export potential. Water scarcity, poor infrastructure, degraded land, a reluctance to adopt new technologies, and security worries are just some of the long-standing challenges that have slowed development.

This section does more than just list the problems; it also explains what those problems mean. Affecting farmers, rural communities, and Afghanistan as a whole, it shows how these problems have an impact on people's daily life. As we gain awareness of the challenges we face, we will be better able to prioritise making the necessary adjustments quickly.

Chapter 5: Building the Necessary Foundations

Afghanistan's agricultural export potential can be unlocked in part through the construction of necessary infrastructure. Investments in transportation, storage, and cold chain facilities are highlighted as a key factor in bridging the gap between rural areas and urban markets and preserving perishable agricultural goods.

This chapter is important because it highlights the role that investment in infrastructure plays in fostering economic expansion. Investment in infrastructure, it argues, is about more than simply buildings; it's also about giving people more agency and helping them earn more money.

Water management and long-term viability constitute Chapter 6.

Water is the lifeblood of agriculture, and this chapter recognises the critical role of water management. Sustainable water management practises may greatly improve agricultural output and resilience, and this report addresses the difficulties of water shortages and the effects of climate change to emphasise their importance.

This chapter's importance goes beyond the realm of agriculture and into that of the larger international conversation about environmental sustainability and responsible resource management. Afghanistan's water management strategy is a good example of how to put sustainability ideas into practise.

Adopting Technology and Expanding Agricultural Education 7

Education in agriculture and the use of cutting-edge tools are the bedrocks of agricultural development. This chapter is helpful in emphasising the significance of training and technology in boosting output and quality. It demonstrates how knowledge and creativity can act as change agents.

This chapter's ramifications are not limited to the territory of Afghanistan. They reaffirm the need of sharing information and developing new tools for agriculture and, by extension, the economy.

Access to Global Markets, Section 8

The development of items isn't enough to unlock Afghanistan's agricultural export potential; access to foreign markets is also necessary. Promotion of Afghan goods, adherence to trade regulations, and the negotiation of trade agreements with importing nations are all topics covered in this chapter. It highlights the significance of international trade and diplomatic relations.

The teachings of this chapter are applicable to countries all over the world because they highlight the importance of trade in promoting economic growth and prosperity. It demonstrates the importance of teamwork and international cooperation in determining the course of economies.

Global Demand for Afghan Agricultural Exports (Chapter 9)

One must be familiar with the global patterns of demand in order to appreciate the importance of Afghanistan's agricultural export potential. The need for unique and organically grown foods is discussed in this chapter. It examines the rise in demand for nutritious, sustainably derived foods and highlights the ways in which Afghanistan may provide such demands

There are two main takeaways from this chapter. The first thing they stress is how critical it is to meet international demand. Second, they bring to light the global trends that Afghanistan might use to its economic advantage.

Case studies and examples of progress are presented in Chapter 10.

This chapter provides a variety of personal accounts that show how opening Afghanistan's agricultural export potential can have a profound impact on the country. It uses actual case studies to demonstrate how Afghan farmers and business owners have improved their communities and the country as a whole by capitalising on agricultural opportunities.

The value of these accounts cannot be overstated. They provide an example of success and proof that agriculture in Afghanistan has the potential to change the country's history for the better.

Conclusion

In conclusion, this analysis is crucial to the growth of Afghanistan's economy. It's a story of perseverance and change. The importance of agriculture as a driving force in the country's pursuit of economic growth and stability is emphasised.

More than just a detailed portrait of Afghanistan's agricultural potential, this study highlights the country's road to renewal. The Afghan people's determination to change their country's narrative and their economic future by realising its vast agricultural export potential is inspiring.

1.3- Provide an overview of the key chapters and themes covered in the book.

An In-Depth Look at Afghanistan's Agricultural Export Potential

Introduction

Providing a road map of the book's key chapters and ideas is essential as we set out on this adventure to discover Afghanistan's agricultural export potential and its consequences for the nation's economic development. The purpose of this introduction is to lay out the analytical landscape we will explore and to emphasise the fundamental ideas that will guide our investigation. These sections are crucial to understanding the nuances of Afghanistan's agriculture industry and the transformative potential it offers.

Afghanistan's Agricultural Heritage (Chapter 1)

In the first section of our book, we explore the long tradition of agriculture in Afghanistan. The rest of the analysis rests on the foundation laid in this chapter. Afghanistan's agricultural identity is traced back to a complex web of past civilizations and agricultural advancements, and this book delves into that history. Our adventure kicks off with a look back at the civilizations of the Indus Valley and the Achaemenid Empire, two ancient powers that had profound impacts on agriculture in Afghanistan. By honouring and learning from this history, we may better appreciate how the past impacts Afghanistan's agricultural present and future.

The Present Agriculture Situation in Afghanistan (Chapter 2)

In the second chapter, we learn all about the current situation in Afghan farming. We look at the current agricultural setting, deconstructing the major crops, difficulties, and prospects that make up it. Providing insight into the predominate crops and their significance in the context of food security, this chapter is essential in providing a solid perspective of the current situation. It's a sobering illustration of the difficulties faced by Afghan farmers due to things like water shortages and a lack of infrastructure. The cornerstone for realising the agriculture sector's unrealized potential in Afghanistan is the identification of growth and development opportunities.

Chapter 3: Products That Could Be Exported

down the third chapter, we hone down on the potential for agricultural exports from Afghanistan. Here, we zero down on the wide variety of goods that are the real secret to the success of American agriculture abroad. Value-added foods and ingredients are the focus of this investigation. Special emphasis is placed on each product to emphasise its salability and distinctive qualities. By concentrating on these prospective export items, we paint a picture of the agricultural revolution that is within reach in Afghanistan. We highlight the products' unique selling characteristics and show how they may compete in foreign markets.

Issues Facing Afghan Farming (Chapter 4)

The enormous difficulties facing Afghan agriculture are discussed in the fourth chapter. Water scarcity, infrastructural gaps, land degradation, slow acceptance of new technologies, and security worries are just some of the issues that are thoroughly examined. Afghan farmers and the communities they sustain are featured prominently in this chapter as a tribute to the power of perseverance in the face of hardship. It's a sobering reminder of the stakes involved in reforming the agricultural sector and the haste with which they must be addressed. The magnitude of these problems helps us see why we need radical, unconventional answers.

Chapter 5: Building the Necessary Foundations

Improving the country's infrastructure is essential to realising the full potential of Afghanistan's agricultural exports. The need of investing in transportation, storage, and cold chain facilities for linking rural areas to markets and preserving agricultural produce is discussed in detail in chapter five. Infrastructure development is not just about physical structures; it is about empowerment and economic prosperity, and this chapter is vital in recognising the tangible dimensions of change. We show that investments in these sectors can help the Afghan people better their standard of living and their economic prospects by underlining the importance of infrastructure development.

Water management and long-term viability constitute Chapter 6.

The sixth chapter focuses on water management and sustainability, two topics crucial to the development of agriculture in Afghanistan. Given the importance of water to agricultural production and cattle husbandry, we focus heavily on this issue. This chapter emphasises the necessity for sustainable water management practises by discussing the difficulties brought on by water scarcity and the effects of climate change. This is a conversation starter about environmental sustainability and ethical resource management on a global scale, not just for Afghanistan. We explore Afghanistan's water management system to show how sustainability ideas might be put into practise.

Adopting Technology and Expanding Agricultural Education 7

In the seventh chapter, we look at how contemporary agricultural education and technology may make a difference. The foundation of agricultural development, these factors are crucial in raising output and improving quality. This chapter emphasises that the transformation of agriculture extends beyond simple cultivation by highlighting the role of information and innovation as drivers for change. It's a process of expanding one's knowledge and adapting to new developments. This chapter's relevance is not limited to Afghanistan; rather, it is reflective of the worldwide value of sharing information and using new technologies to advance agriculture and, by extension, economies.

Access to Global Markets, Section 8

Access to foreign markets is essential to unlock Afghanistan's agricultural export potential, which requires more than just growing products. We go into the complexity of promoting Afghan products, maintaining compliance with trade regulations, and creating trade agreements with importing countries in Chapter 8. Globalisation and economic diplomacy are given more attention in this chapter. It demonstrates how economies are intertwined and how trade is vital to economic growth. Beyond the borders of Afghanistan, the lessons learned in this section are a testament to the impact that teamwork and international cooperation can have on economic outcomes.

Global Demand for Afghan Agricultural Exports (Chapter 9)

Understanding Afghanistan's agricultural export potential requires an in-depth understanding of global dynamics and demand, as is highlighted in Chapter Nine. The need for unique and organically grown foods is discussed in this chapter. It examines the rise in demand for nutritious, sustainably derived foods and highlights the ways in which Afghanistan may provide such demands. These repercussions are not limited to Afghanistan; rather, they echo throughout nations and highlight the interconnection of economies and the significance of commerce in promoting prosperity. It demonstrates the need of synchronising output with international demand and capitalising on global tendencies.

Case studies and examples of progress are presented in Chapter 10.

Our analysis concludes with a discussion of real-world examples. We demonstrate the transforming effect of realising Afghanistan's agricultural export potential through a series of case studies and success stories. These examples are more than just anecdotes; they show how agriculture in Afghanistan has the capacity to change the country's history. They serve as examples of the positive change brought about by the agricultural revolution in rural areas and the country as a whole. Sharing these accounts is a way of honouring the hard work and determination of farmers and businesspeople in Afghanistan who have used their talents to improve their villages and the country as a whole.

Conclusion

As we wrap off this summary, it's important to recall the book's overarching goal: to stress the critical nature of recognising and capitalising on Afghanistan's agricultural export potential. It's a nod to the importance of farming to the nation's economy and political stability. This in-depth look at the Afghan people's perseverance and strength is a source of inspiration. An investigation of agriculture's transformative potential and a tribute to the resilience of the Afghan people as they realise the full economic and cultural potential of their country's agricultural exports. The trip is a profound recognition of the transformative potential latent in the soil of Afghanistan, ready to be released for the betterment of its people and its nation.

global community.

Chapter 2:
A Look Back at the Farming in Afghanistan

2.1- Explore Afghanistan's historical agricultural legacy, including its ancient civilizations and agricultural practices.

The Agricultural Heritage of Afghanistan's Past

Introduction

Agriculture in Afghanistan has a long and storied history, dating back millennia despite the country's varied topography (from the Hindu Kush to the Amu Darya). In this first part of our adventure, we will delve into this complex web of past events. This article delves into Afghanistan's rich agricultural history, which serves as a cornerstone for the country's agricultural present and future. The relevance of this historical overview can only be grasped by delving into the depths of time and learning about the agricultural customs that have moulded the Afghan environment.

The origin of ancient civilizations is discussed in Section 1.1.

The rise of ancient civilizations is inextricably intertwined with Afghanistan's agricultural history. Parts of modern-day Afghanistan were formerly home to the Indus Valley Civilization, one of the first urban centres in human history. This ancient culture farmed the land to produce a bountiful harvest of cereals, beans, and other crops. Understanding the origins of Afghan agriculture requires looking into the agricultural practises of this civilization.

Agriculture under the Achaemenid Empire is discussed in Section 1.2.

Agricultural progress in the area owes a great deal to the administrative expertise of the Achaemenid Empire. Darius the Great, a monarch of Persia, enacted a number of measures designed to better organise and enhance agricultural output. Land surveys, canal building, and the establishment of uniform grain measurement standards were all part of his policy agenda. These changes represent some of the oldest examples of agricultural planning and management in the area, and they were crucial to the expansion of agricultural production.

Section 1.3: Agriculture in Ancient Afghanistan

We then shift our focus to the traditional farming methods that have emerged in the Afghanistan region throughout the years. This section looks at the crops grown, the methods used, and the inventions developed as a result of the local climate and geography. Afghan farming produced a wide variety of crops, from wheat and barley to grapes and pomegranates.

"Section 1.4: Irrigation, Afghanistan's Economic Backbone"

The history of irrigation in Afghanistan's fields is significant. Like their forebears, the ancient Afghans used complex irrigation systems to make use of the region's plentiful rivers and streams. This technology not only helped people grow food, but it also aided in the development of complex societies. To fully grasp the irrigation systems of Afghanistan in the present day, one must be familiar with their history, methods, and advancements.

Section 1.5: Agricultural Trade and the Silk Road

Afghan farming was significantly influenced by the Silk Road, the famous network of trade routes that traversed Asia. This section delves into the ways in which the Silk Road influenced the farming methods used in Afghanistan. This section explains how the trade routes promoted agricultural interaction, from the dissemination of new crop varieties like rice to the dissemination of irrigation techniques.

Agriculture's History and Its Present Importance

The chapter ends with reiterating the importance of Afghanistan's agricultural heritage throughout the years. Afghan agriculture is still heavily influenced by the ancient civilizations' agricultural practises and technological advances. Recognising the ageless wisdom ingrained in Afghan soil requires more than a superficial understanding of this legacy.

Conclusion

The groundwork for our future investigations into Afghanistan's agricultural history has been laid in this first chapter. It's a recognition of how much the ancient civilizations, agricultural advancements, and trade along the Silk Road influenced agriculture in Afghanistan. Afghan agriculture has a long and illustrious history, full with lessons that can inform the country's present and future. It serves as a timely reminder that history is not a museum piece, but rather a treasure trove of insights and ideas that can be used to build a stronger agricultural industry and a more successful country.

2.2- Discuss the impact of historical events and conflicts on the country's agricultural sector.

Chapter 2: The Impact of Conflicts and Historical Events on Afghanistan's Agricultural Sector is a Complicated Web.

Introduction

Afghanistan's agricultural sector bears the unmistakable stamp of the nation's turbulent past, which was distinguished by a complex interplay of historical events and battles. From the invasions of Alexander the Great through the Soviet-Afghan War, this chapter delves into the complicated web of historical events that have shaped and interrupted agricultural practises in Afghanistan. It demonstrates how politics, war, and the lives of Afghan farmers are all intertwined.

The Influence of Alexander the Great on the Development of Agriculture

Starting in the 4th century BCE, when Alexander the Great invaded Afghanistan, we learn how that event changed the agricultural landscape of the region forever. Greek colonisation of Afghanistan resulted in an influx of new plant varieties and farming methods. This chapter explores the role of the Hellenistic period in agriculture and how it established the groundwork for the modern practise of crop diversification.

Cultural interaction along the Silk Road (Section 2.2)

Agriculture in Afghanistan owes a great deal to the Silk Road, which connected the region to other parts of the world. This section delves into the ways in which the Silk Road promoted the sharing of agricultural goods, techniques, and information. The outcome was a synthesis of farming practises that are still useful in Afghanistan today, such as the widespread adoption of rice and modern irrigation systems.

Disruption to agriculture due to Mongol invasions is discussed in Section 2.3.

Agriculture in Afghanistan suffered greatly as a result of the Mongol invasions in the 13th century. As a result of the destruction wrought by the invasions, agricultural output fell. However, the Mongols also contributed to agriculture in the region by introducing novel techniques and crops, such as drought-resistant barley. The turbulent period of Mongol control and its complicated aftermath are explored in this section.

Section 2.4: "The Mughal Empire and the Flowering of Agriculture"

When the Mughal Empire arrived in Afghanistan in the 16th century, they brought with them a time of peace and agricultural prosperity. The Mughals fostered the production of high-value commodities such as saffron and pomegranates, and their control left a lasting imprint in the Afghan agricultural environment. Learn how the Mughal era contributed to the growth of the agricultural sector in Afghanistan.

The Great Game and International Influence (Section 2.5)

The "Great Game," a geopolitical rivalry between the British and Russian Empires, centred on Afghanistan in the 19th century. This section looks at the impact on Afghan agriculture of outside interference, political manoeuvring, and the imposition of agreements and treaties. Land ownership and agricultural practises are examined in relation to these geopolitical developments.

Disruption to Agriculture Caused by the Soviet-Afghan War (Section 2.6)

The Soviet-Afghan War was the most recent major conflict to have an impact on agriculture in Afghanistan. This section examines how the conflict, which lasted from 1979 to 1989, affected agriculture by causing severe damage to irrigation infrastructure, forcing the relocation of rural people, and displacing farmers. The destruction of infrastructure and the prevalence of landmines are two war legacies that continue to hinder agriculture in Afghanistan.

The Opium Trade and the Time of the Taliban (Section 2.7)

The emergence of the Taliban in the 1990s had a complex influence on Afghan agriculture. The Taliban rule banned some farming methods but encouraged others, such as opium production. This had a profound impact on agricultural policy. This analysis considers how the Taliban regime affected agriculture in Afghanistan, focusing on the country's centrality in the opium trade.

Substituting Crops During Conflicts

Traditional crops have often been replaced with others that are more hardy in times of conflict. This section describes how the prolonged conflict in Afghanistan has led farmers to switch to growing different, often more profitable crops.

Afghan farmers' adaptability and resilience is discussed in Section 2.9.

In light of Afghanistan's troubled past, it's important to give credit to the country's farmers for showing extraordinary fortitude and flexibility. In spite of natural disasters, wars, and other setbacks, the people commemorated here have persisted in cultivating the land.

Conclusion

Afghanistan's agriculture industry has a long and complicated history that this chapter explores. It shows how war and other external and internal factors have altered agricultural practises in Afghanistan. It is significant because it honours the tenacity of Afghan farmers who, despite decades of turmoil, have managed to keep their farms running and provide for their families. Acquiring this historical perspective helps place current agricultural activities and development ideas in their proper perspective. This chapter serves as a reminder that Afghanistan's history is more than just a record of war and bloodshed; it is also a tribute to the resilience and fortitude of a people who are inextricably linked to their homeland and the enduring heritage of their agricultural traditions.

Chapter 3:
The Present Agriculture Situation in Afghanistan

3.1- Analyze the current state of Afghanistan's agriculture, focusing on key crops, challenges, and opportunities.

State of Agriculture in Afghanistan: An Evaluation

Introduction

Understanding the current situation of agriculture in Afghanistan is crucial before entering into the complex realm of Afghanistan's prospective agricultural exports. This chapter provides the framework for evaluating the current state of affairs, including the most important crops grown, the most pressing problems, and the most promising future prospects. It's fundamental to grasping the background upon which we hope to create an image of metamorphosis.

Afghanistan's Primary Crops (Section 3.1)

Many different crops, each with its own history and value, form the basis of Afghan agriculture. This section provides an in-depth analysis of the most important crops grown in the country. We analyse the agricultural environment down to its smallest details, from the staple cereals like wheat, maize, and barley to the high-value crops like pomegranates, almonds, saffron, and numerous spices. We discuss these crops' potential in domestic and international markets, as well as their economic and nutritional value.

Section 3.2: Problems Facing Afghanistan's Agricultural Sector

Many obstacles stand in the way of progress in Afghanistan's agriculture industry. Here, we take a critical look at these problems, painting a full picture of the difficulties Afghan farmers endure. We break down the problems that have plagued agriculture in Afghanistan for decades, including water scarcity, climate change's effects, land degradation, infrastructure gaps, and the imperative to adopt modern technologies. We also investigate the social and economic effects of these difficulties on rural areas and the nation as a whole.

Opportunities for expansion and improvement are discussed in Section 3.3.

Despite difficulties, the agriculture sector in Afghanistan offers some opportunities and signs of promise. This segment elucidates the economic sectors where the country has the greatest potential for growth and development. Afghan agriculture's unrealized potential is investigated, with special focus on openings for crop diversification, export-oriented farming, and the implementation of cutting-edge technology to boost output and quality. By exploring what might be, we find the opportunities that could revolutionise agriculture, improve farmers' incomes, and aid in Afghanistan's economic revival.

Section 3.4: The Importance of Ecologically Sound Methods

Modern agriculture is increasingly focused on sustainability, and Afghanistan is no different. In this piece, we'll look at how sustainable farming practises can help farmers in Afghanistan weather tough times and protect the environment at the same time. We examine the current agricultural landscape and the possibility for sustainable agriculture, organic farming, and responsible resource management to alleviate some of the pressing difficulties faced by farmers in Afghanistan.

The Afghan Farmer and His or Her Resolve, Section 3.5

The indomitable spirit and ingenuity of Afghan farmers must be included in any discussion about agriculture in Afghanistan. This piece is dedicated to the hardy souls who, despite hardships, keep ploughing the fields and feeding their communities. We discuss the hardships they've faced, the ways in which they've adapted, and the bright futures they envision thanks to advances in agriculture.

Conclusion

This section lays the groundwork for further research on the agricultural situation in Afghanistan. It sheds light on the foundational crops that support the industry, the numerous obstacles that have stymied its development, and the promising new directions that are opening up. It highlights the significance of knowing the current state of affairs in order to chart a path forward for development and expansion. Despite the many obstacles, there is reason to be optimistic about agriculture in Afghanistan because of the perseverance of Afghan farmers, the possibility of more sustainable practises, and the growth chances. To picture a future in which agriculture in Afghanistan thrives and drives the country's economic rebirth and prosperity, we must first understand the dynamics of Afghan agriculture today.

3.2- Discuss the challenges such as water scarcity, infrastructure deficiencies, and security concerns.

Issues with Water, Infrastructure, and Safety in Afghan Agriculture

Introduction

Understanding the agriculture industry in Afghanistan requires a thorough examination of the significant obstacles it faces. In this section, we'll take a close look at the factors that have slowed agriculture's progress in Afghanistan. We take a close look at the industry's most pressing problems, including a lack of water, inadequate infrastructure, and security threats. We hope that by breaking down these obstacles, more people will gain an understanding of the complexities of Afghanistan's agricultural landscape.

Water scarcity, the lifeblood of agriculture, is discussed in Section 4.1.

Agriculture in Afghanistan relies heavily on water, making water management a top priority. This section dives into the problems caused by water shortage, focusing on the limited availability of water and the issues of delivering water for irrigation. The effects of water scarcity on agriculture, livestock, and rural economies are discussed. In addition, we acknowledge the importance of sustainable water management practises in boosting agricultural output and resilience.

Disadvantages in Agriculture's Core Infrastructure (Section 4.2)

A reliable system for moving and storing crops is the backbone of the agricultural industry. Yet, Afghanistan has severe gaps in this area. Inadequate infrastructure, including roads, warehouses, and cold storage, all contribute to the problems discussed here. The effects of these shortcomings on postharvest losses, market access, and crop preservation are examined. Infrastructure development is highlighted as a key enabler of economic growth and better living conditions.

Concerns for Safety and Possible Conflict Imperatives

Because of decades of war and instability, agriculture in Afghanistan is plagued by fear for its safety. From landmines and insurgent activity to the broader repercussions of violence on rural communities, this section provides a comprehensive assessment of the security difficulties encountered by farmers. It highlights the ways in which security issues have affected land ownership and the long-term viability of agricultural livelihoods by forcing people to flee their homes.

Land degradation: a "silent crisis," according to Section 4.4.

A hidden but ubiquitous catastrophe, land degradation threatens Afghanistan's agricultural future. Soil erosion, salinization, and desertification are just few of the forms of land degradation discussed here. Here, we examine how degraded land reduces agricultural output, posing a hazard to global food supplies. To address this problem, sustainable land management practises are also emphasised.

Crop-threatening insects and diseases are discussed in Section 4.5.

There is always the risk of pests and diseases destroying Afghan crops. Challenges posed by agricultural pests and diseases are explored here, with a particular emphasis on how they affect wheat and other staple crops. We look at the monetary effects of these problems and discuss methods for controlling pests and preventing diseases.

Adopting New Technologies: The Digital Divide

Although it is essential for increasing output and product quality, the implementation of modern agricultural technology confronts obstacles in Afghanistan. This section highlights the information and technology gap that exists in rural areas, where many farmers lack access to modern tools and resources. It analyses the challenges associated with adopting new technologies and stresses the importance of measures to overcome these obstacles and equip farmers in Afghanistan with the resources they need to succeed.

Inequalities in the Economy that Threaten Farm Viability are discussed in Section 4.7.

The profitability of farming is undermined by economic inequalities both within and between rural communities. This section examines the difficulties encountered by smallholder farmers, including the gaps in their access to resources, markets, and loans. It highlights the importance of inclusive policies that help all sectors of the agricultural community and the significance of these inequities for agricultural development.

Conclusion

This chapter looks deeply into the problems that plague agriculture in Afghanistan, from a lack of water and infrastructure to the threat of war and insecurity. It emphasises the complexity and interconnectedness of these problems, recognising that solving them will require a broad strategy. To reform Afghan agriculture and realise its potential, we must first have an appreciation for the severe challenges it faces. By acknowledging the importance of these problems, we move closer to a vision in which agriculture in Afghanistan thrives, rural communities prosper, and the country's economy is revitalised and stabilised.

3.3- Highlight potential areas for growth and development.

Developing Afghanistan's Agricultural Sector: Chapter 5

Introduction

Despite the many obstacles facing Afghanistan's agricultural sector, the country's agricultural sector has tremendous growth and development prospects. This chapter focuses on identifying promising regions for agricultural development in Afghanistan. We explore the unrealized potential in the industry by focusing on the chances for crop diversification, export-oriented agriculture, and the implementation of novel techniques to boost output and quality. By focusing on and developing these promising avenues, we can hope to restore agriculture in Afghanistan and help the country's economy recover.

Crop diversification: expanding one's horizons; Section 5.1

Increasing crop diversity is essential for agricultural development in Afghanistan. The possibility for increasing the variety of crops grown in the country is investigated here. We take a look at how diversification can improve food security, lessen exposure to climate-related shocks, and open up new avenues for high-value, export-oriented crops. We show the transformative potential of increasing crop options through case studies and instances of effective agricultural diversification.

High-Value Crops with Export Potential, Section 5.2

Afghanistan's agricultural sector has a great deal of room to expand thanks to the production of high-value crops. Here we highlight some of the most promising export crops, such as pomegranates, almonds, saffron, and other spices. In this article, we explore the distinctive qualities of these crops, the demand for them in the market, and their potential to propel Afghan agriculture into the international scene. We can imagine a future when agricultural products from Afghanistan are sought after on international markets if we learn to maximise the potential of high-value crops.

Section 5.3: "Innovation and Technology: Advancing Farmer Self-Sufficiency"

Increased agricultural output and product quality in Afghanistan can be attributed in large part to the country's openness to and use of new technologies. This article delves into how new tools, such as precision agriculture and ICT, have altered conventional farming methods. We highlight effective programmes that have improved farmers' access to information and resources in Afghanistan, stressing the importance of computer literacy and the part played by innovation in agricultural progress.

Environment preservation and sustainable practises are discussed in Section 5.4.

Agriculture in Afghanistan is a vital sector of the country's economy, and sustainability is not just a concept. Sustainable agriculture, organic farming, and wise use of resources are all explored in this area. Sustainable practises, such as conserving water and increasing soil fertility, are highlighted as having positive effects on the environment and the economy. Sustainable practises protect the environment and give Afghan farmers a leg up on the competition.

Section 5.5: Export-Driven Agriculture and Internationalisation

The expansion of agricultural production relies heavily on access to foreign markets. In this paragraph, we will discuss the significance of export-oriented agriculture and the significance of synchronising production with global demand. We discuss the challenges of marketing Afghan agricultural goods, monitoring for trade regulatory compliance, and negotiating trade deals with countries that are looking to import Afghan goods. Growing Afghanistan's exports is a key step towards the country's economic development and globalisation.

A Catalyst for Growth: Section 5.6: Empowering Women in Agriculture

Gender equality is an issue, but empowering women in agriculture can also spur economic development in the sector. This section elucidates the crucial roles that Afghan women have played in agriculture and showcases programmes that encourage their participation. Recognising and empowering women's contributions in agriculture can lead to enormous economic and social benefits.

Cooperative farming and farmer associations are a great way to strengthen the local community (see Section 5.7).

Organising farmers into cooperatives and associations can do wonders for the agriculture sector. The advantages of farmers working together, exchanging information, and pooling resources are discussed here. The importance of these groups in bolstering rural communities and raising agricultural output is highlighted.
Conclusion

This section shines a light on the potential for improvement in Afghanistan's agricultural sector. These futures show a vision of transition in farming, from crop diversification to high-value crops, innovation, sustainability, and farming with an eye towards export. By focusing on and developing these promising sectors, we may imagine a future in which agriculture in Afghanistan thrives, rural communities prosper, and the country's economy is revitalised and stabilised. This is not some far-off fantasy but a real possibility; it's how Afghan agriculture may become a pillar of the country's economic success.

Chapter 4:
Products That Could Be Exported

4.1- Examine the agricultural products with export potential, including fruits, nuts, saffron, spices, herbs, wool, and medicinal plants.

Afghanistan's export potential is explored in Chapter 6: Nurturing Afghanistan's Bounty.

Introduction

Afghan agriculture is a hidden treasure waiting to be discovered by the world. Here, we explore in detail the wide variety of agricultural items that have tremendous export potential. Afghanistan is home to a plethora of high-quality goods that might be exported to other countries, including delicious fruits, valuable saffron threads, aromatic spices, flavorful meats, and crunchy nuts. Herbs, wool, and medicinal plants are also explored in detail, as are their prospective uses and market demand. By highlighting these goods, we show the potential for change in Afghanistan's agricultural sector.

Afghan Fruits: Sample Some of Nature's Abundance

Fruits are abundant in Afghanistan, and each has its own unique taste and market potential. Pomegranates, apricots, figs, grapes, and apples are only few of the fruit types whose export potential is discussed below. We evaluate Afghan fruits for their potential as high-value exports by looking at their quality, demand, and worldwide appeal. We show how to get from the orchard to the global market by using case studies and success stories.

Nutty treats: Afghanistan's nut bounty is discussed in Section 6.2.

Afghanistan is known for its high-quality and delicious nuts, and its exports are much sought for. Here, we highlight the international demand for Afghan nuts and reveal their export potential. We explore the growing, roasting, packaging, and selling stages of nut production to shed light on the value chain that turns these raw materials into marketable commodities.

Section 6.3: Saffron, Afghanistan's Red Gold

Saffron, also known as "red gold," is a highly sought-after and lucrative crop in Afghanistan. This article describes the processes involved in growing, harvesting, and preparing saffron, giving the reader a taste of the care that goes into making this precious spice. The demand and opportunity for Afghan saffron to carve out a premium export niche are highlighted as we investigate the global saffron market.

Flavouring the World with Spices and Culinary Herbs Section 6.4

Afghan coriander, cumin, and mint, among other spices and herbs, have the potential to spice up dishes all over the world. Here, we analyse the potential for exporting these aromatic gems, placing special emphasis on their use in cooking and medicine. We also discuss the international commerce of spices and herbs, promoting Afghanistan as a supplier of premium organic seasonings.

Wool, the fleece and fibre of the Afghan people. Section 6.5.

Afghanistan's textile sector relies heavily on wool, a traditional agricultural crop. This article examines the viability of Afghan wool as an export product, with special focus on the high quality of the wool and the use of time-honored production techniques. We explore the varied uses of wool around the world in the fashion and textile industries.

Natural remedies from plants are discussed in detail in Section 6.6.

There is a wide variety of medicinal plants with various effects in Afghanistan. Here, we discuss the possibility of exporting these therapeutic plants, highlighting their importance in the pharmaceutical and wellness industries. To ensure the proper use and protection of medicinal plants, we also investigate methods of sustainable harvesting and processing.

Case studies and examples of success can be found in Section 6.7.

We present a selection of case studies and success stories to illustrate the possibilities for export of various agricultural products. In these accounts, we meet real Afghan farmers and businesspeople who are capitalising on the export potential of their goods. These examples are more than just anecdotes; they show how agriculture in Afghanistan has the capacity to change the country's history.

Conclusion

Afghanistan is a treasure trove of untapped export potential when it comes to agricultural goods. Afghanistan's agricultural bounty is a well-kept secret that deserves global recognition, including the juicy fruits that grace its orchards, the precious saffron threads that weave a crimson tapestry, the aromatic spices that flavour its cuisine, and the bountiful nuts that add crunch to its markets. Herbs, wool, and medicinal plants all have the ability to contribute to this story of plenty. We show the potential for agricultural reform in Afghanistan by shining a focus on these crops' export potential. It's a dream to see Afghan agriculture flourish to the point that its products are sought after on global markets, boosting the economy, giving voice to farmers, and leaving a legacy of quality.

4.2- Provide in-depth information on each product, such as production, quality, and market demand.

Afghan Fruits: Sample Some of Nature's Abundance

Introduction

Afghanistan's climate and fertile soils allow for the growth of a wide variety of fruits that are known for their juiciness and flavour. Here, we set out on an adventure across Afghanistan's fruit fields to investigate the country's potential as an exporter of its produce. Afghan fruits are a taste of nature's wealth, ranging from pomegranates bursting with ruby-red seeds to apricots that reflect the essence of summer to figs that transport you to Mediterranean climes to apples that are crisp and refreshing. We investigate how these tasty snacks are made and sold in the market today.

Pomegranates, the Crown Jewels of Afghan Orchards, are discussed in Section 6.1.1.

Afghanistan's pomegranates are a highly sought-after export item and among the country's most beloved fruits. Pomegranate cultivation is discussed here, with an emphasis on optimal growing conditions. We take a look at the taste, colour, and overall quality of Afghan pomegranates. We also look at the pomegranate market internationally, highlighting the fruit's worth as a food item and a raw material for other products.

Apricots, the quintessential summer fruit, are discussed in Section 6.1.2.

The apricots of Afghanistan epitomise the season because of their fragrant, sugary flesh. This section explores the apricot harvest, focusing on key producing areas. We investigate the taste, texture, and potential for drying of Afghan apricots. We also look into the fresh and dried apricot markets in Afghanistan because of their potential as lucrative exports.

Section 6.1.3: Figs, a Mediterranean Delight

The warm weather in Afghanistan is perfect for growing figs, which have a honeyed taste and velvety texture. The production of figs, including the cultivated types and their geographic distribution, is discussed in this section. We investigate the taste and texture of Afghan figs, focusing on their fresh eating and drying possibilities. To further establish Afghan figs as a distinct product with international appeal, we also research the worldwide demand for figs.

Apples are crisp and refreshing; see Section 6.1.4.

Apples, with their refreshing crunch and sweet flavour, are a common sight in Afghan orchards. In this part, we examine apple orchards and the many types grown there. We take a look at how good Afghan apples are, paying special attention to their taste, appearance, and potential for long-term storage. We also look into the possibility for exporting Afghan apples and the demand for these apples in international markets.

Opportunity in the Grapevine (Section 6.1.5)

Afghanistan has a long history of cultivating grapes for many purposes, including as table grapes, raisins, and wine. In this section, we'll look at the grape harvest and discuss the best places to grow grapes. We look at the characteristics of Afghan grapes, including their taste, size, and versatility. We also explore the demand for Afghan grapes, which we promote as an export-oriented product with a deep cultural history.

Nutty treats: Afghanistan's nut bounty is discussed in Section 6.2.

Introduction

Afghanistan's nuts are highly sought after due to their deliciousness and high quality. Here we examine the supply, quality, and consumer demand for several nuts grown in Afghanistan. These tasty nuts are highly prized not only for their delicious flavour but also for the many ways they can be used in the kitchen. We investigate where nuts are grown, how they're harvested and processed, and why people all across the world crave their delicious and healthy products.

Almonds are a nutritional powerhouse, as is discussed in Section 6.2.1.

Because of their high nutrient content and delicious flavour, almonds have gained widespread popularity. In this part, we look at the almond industry in Afghanistan, highlighting the most productive areas. We focus on the taste, size, and nutritional value of Afghan almonds to evaluate their quality. We also look into the potential for exporting Afghan almonds as a product with broad appeal.

Pistachios, the "Green Gold" of Afghanistan, are discussed in Section 6.2.2.

Pistachios are considered the "green gold" of Afghanistan due to their high value and exceptional taste. This section discusses the cultivation and harvesting of pistachios, focusing on the key growing areas. The unique flavour, large size, and vibrant green colour of Afghan pistachios are discussed, along with other aspects of their excellence. We also look at the pistachio market in Afghanistan, where the nuts are considered a premium export.

Nuts Are Good for Your Heart, Section 6.2.3

Walnuts' rich, nutty flavour and beneficial effects on the heart have earned them widespread acclaim. This section discusses the nut-growing regions of Afghanistan, as well as the production of walnuts in the country as a whole. We focus on the taste, size, and nutritional benefits of Afghan walnuts to evaluate their quality. We also look into the demand for Afghan walnuts, which we see as an opportunity to sell a product that is gaining in popularity around the world.

Section 6.3: Saffron, Afghanistan's Red Gold

Introduction

Saffron, also known as "red gold," is a highly sought-after and lucrative crop in Afghanistan. Here, we delve into the cultivation, quality, and popularity of Afghan saffron on the global market. Growing saffron is not only a time-honored custom, but also a lucrative business. We go into the intricate harvesting and processing procedures for saffron, highlighting the qualities that define Afghan saffron apart. We also analyse the global saffron market, with a focus on Afghanistan's saffron and its potential as a niche export.

Saffron cultivation has a long history of success and is discussed in detail in Section 6.3.1.

Afghanistan has a rich history of saffron growing and is widely recognised as a source of the world's finest saffron. In this section, we examine saffron cultivation, paying special attention to its natural habitats. The vibrant colour, powerful perfume, and robust flavour of Afghan saffron are all factors we consider. We also explore the global demand for Afghan saffron, which we promote as a luxury item with a long and storied history.

Saffron harvesting and processing is a labour of love, as described in Section 6.3.2.

Saffron is harvested and processed with great care and attention to detail, a testament to the hard work and perseverance of Afghan farmers. This section delves into the processes involved in gathering and preparing saffron, with an emphasis on those that help maintain the spice's integrity. Here, we delve into the history and cultural significance of Afghan saffron, focusing on its use as a sought-after spice and natural medicine.

Flavouring the World with Spices and Culinary Herbs Section 6.4

Introduction

Afghan coriander, cumin, and mint, among other spices and herbs, have the potential to spice up dishes all over the world. Production, Quality, and Other Aspects are Discussed

 and the thirst of consumers for these scented gems. The culinary and therapeutic uses of spices and herbs have contributed to their monetary value. We explore where they are grown, how they are harvested and processed, and their value in culinary and medical markets around the world.

The Aromatic Spice and Herb Coriander (Section 6.4.1)

Coriander has a unique lemony flavour and can be used as both a spice and a herb. Here we look at the cultivation of coriander in Afghanistan and the specific provinces where it is produced. We analyse the characteristics of Afghan coriander, paying special attention to its flavour, aroma, and culinary value. We also look into the demand for Afghan coriander as a potential export spice and herb.

For the earthy and fragrant spice, see Section 6.4.2, "Cumin."

The earthy, fragrant spice cumin is used in a wide variety of dishes. In this part, we examine the growing areas that are responsible for the majority of Afghanistan's cumin production. We investigate

Afghan cumin, focusing on its qualities as an aromatic spice with a wide range of culinary applications. We also look into the demand for Afghan cumin, promoting it as a desirable spice in export markets.

Mint, an aromatic culinary herb; see Section 6.4.3.

Mint is a popular herb used in cooking because of its refreshing flavour and enticing scent. Here we take a closer look at mint cultivation in Afghanistan, focusing on the most fruitful growing areas. We go into the attributes of Afghan mint, including its flavour, scent, and culinary uses. As a multipurpose plant with international appeal, we also explore the market for Afghan mint.

Wool, the fleece and fibre of the Afghan people. Section 6.5.

Introduction

Afghanistan's textile sector relies heavily on wool, a traditional agricultural crop. In this article, we'll take a look at Afghan wool's supply, quality, and consumer demand. In addition to its practical uses in clothing and home decor, wool is also prized for its aesthetic qualities as an element in fashion and textiles. We examine where in Afghanistan wool is grown, how it's sheared and processed, and why that matters for the global textile industry.

Section 6.5.1: Wool Manufacturing, The Shearing Tradition

Afghanistan's rural communities have a long and storied history of wool production. This section examines the wool-making process, focusing on well-known sheep and goat-rearing areas. The quality of Afghan wool is discussed, with special attention paid to the wool's warmth, tenderness, and inherent colour variations. Furthermore, we research the demand for Afghan wool, emphasising its value as a flexible and long-lasting material.

Processing Wool: From Fleece to Fabric (Section 6.5.2)

In Afghanistan, wool is processed using age-old techniques that take raw fleece and turn it into cloth. In this part, we examine the processes used to prepare wool, focusing on those that help maintain the wool's original qualities without altering it. We examine the relevance of Afghan wool in the textile industry, focusing on its uses in clothing, rugs, and other handmade goods.

Natural remedies from plants are discussed in detail in Section 6.6.

Introduction

There is a wide variety of medicinal plants with various effects in Afghanistan. In this article, we will discuss the supply, quality, and demand for these therapeutic herbs. There is a lot of money to be made in the pharmaceutical and wellness businesses thanks to medicinal plants' restorative capabilities. We investigate where in Afghanistan medicinal plants are grown, how they are harvested and processed, and why they are so important to international trade.

Section 6.6.1: The Healing Power of Medicinal Plants

Both the soil and the people of Afghanistan benefit from the cultivation of therapeutic plants. In this section, we examine medicinal plant production, focusing on areas that are well-known for the growth of such plants. We focus on the potency and purity of Afghan medicinal plants as we evaluate their quality. We also look into the demand for Afghan medicinal plants, highlighting their potential as useful resources for the pharmaceutical and wellness businesses.

Section 6.6.2: Responsible Harvesting and Processing

In Afghanistan, laws and regulations ensure that medicinal plants are collected and processed in a sustainable manner. This section delves into sustainable harvesting and processing practises, with an emphasis on procedures that protect the quality and medicinal efficacy of Afghan medicinal plants. We look at how these plants have been used for healing purposes both historically and today, with an emphasis on how they have been used in contemporary medicine.

Conclusion

In this part, you'll find specifics about the production, quality, and market demand for each agricultural commodity. The cultivation, quality qualities, and place in worldwide markets for everything from fruits and nuts to saffron, spices, herbs, wool, and medicinal plants is different. We provide a full picture of Afghanistan's agricultural wealth by illuminating its production and export potential for various items. These goods have the potential to improve the economy, give farmers more control over their own lives, and make an impact on a worldwide scale; they also increase agricultural diversity in the country.

Chapter 5:
Problems Facing Afghan Farming

5.1- Explore the challenges faced by Afghan farmers, including land degradation, limited technology adoption, and the need for improved irrigation.

Chapter 7: The Obstacles Facing Afghan Farmers (When Translated)

Introduction

Farmers in Afghanistan encounter numerous difficulties due to the country's unique topography and turbulent past. In this chapter, we look at the difficulties Afghan farmers face in their search for a living. Farmers in Afghanistan face a wide range of difficult problems, including erosion of their fields due to land degradation, a lack of adoption of modern technology that would increase output, a dire need for better irrigation systems, and the ever-present danger of pests and diseases. The effects of these problems on rural areas and the economy as a whole are examined in this section.

The Silent Crisis of Land Degradation, Section 7.1

Afghan agriculture is beset by a subtle but ubiquitous crisis: land degradation. Soil erosion, salinization, and desertification are just a few examples of the problems caused by land degradation, which we explore here. We investigate how land degradation affects agricultural output and emphasise the danger it poses to food security. We also stress the importance of sustainable land management practises in addressing this problem and protecting Afghanistan's rich agricultural heritage.

The Digital Divide and Limited Technology Adoption Section 7.2

Improved output and quality are two outcomes directly attributable to the use of cutting-edge agriculture technology. We examine the low rate of technology use in Afghan farming to illustrate the digital divide in the country's rural areas. A lack of digital literacy and other informational and material barriers are among those we investigate. We also stress the importance of measures that help Afghan farmers gain access to education and resources.

Irrigation Problems: Managing Limited Supplies of Water

Afghanistan faces difficulties in irrigation due to a lack of water and inadequate infrastructure, which hinders the country's ability to cultivate crops. Here, we discuss the difficulties of obtaining and distributing water for agricultural purposes, as well as the importance of better irrigation systems. We look at how low levels of irrigation affect harvests and people's ability to make a living in the countryside. In order to boost agricultural output and stability, we also stress the significance of sustainable water management practises.

Crop-threatening insects and diseases are discussed in Section 7.4.

Both basic and high-value crops in Afghanistan are always at risk from pests and diseases. Here, we look into the difficulties posed by agricultural pests and illnesses, specifically how they affect crop production. We take a look at the monetary effects of these obstacles, highlighting their role in increasing production costs and decreasing yield. In order to protect agricultural output, we also investigate methods of pest and disease management and prevention.

Inequalities in the Economy That Threaten Farm Viability Section 7.5

The viability of agriculture in Afghanistan is threatened by economic gaps both within and between farming communities. Here, we examine the discrepancies in people's access to materials, markets, and finance. Given their lack of financial and political clout, smallholder farmers and other marginalised groups present unique issues that we investigate. We also highlight the implications of these differences for agricultural growth and the need for equitable policies that benefit all sectors of the agricultural community.

Agriculture's Dark Side: Sec. 7.6 "Insecurity and Conflict"

Conflict and insecurity have put a long, ominous shadow on agriculture in Afghanistan. Security threats, such as landmines and insurgent activity, as well as the broader repercussions of conflict on rural populations are discussed here. We investigate the impact that security issues have had on land ownership and the long-term viability of agricultural livelihoods, as well as on the disruption of farming practises. We also stress the need of interventions designed to lessen the toll of violence and instability on rural communities.

A Worsening Climate Threat, Section 7.7

The stability of Afghan agriculture is threatened by a new threat: climate change. Here, we look into how climate change will affect farming, water supplies, and animals. We look at how frequent weather disasters affect food supplies and rural economies. Furthermore, we stress the significance of adaptation techniques to strengthen resistance to climate change and secure agriculture in Afghanistan's future.

Conclusion

Recognising the intricacy and interconnectedness of the obstacles faced by Afghan farmers, this chapter provides guidance on how to traverse this landscape. Afghanistan's agricultural landscape is shaped by a number of factors, including land degradation, low technology adoption, irrigation difficulties, pests and diseases, economic inequality, insecurity and violence, and climate change. By identifying and analysing these massive challenges, we can develop the strategies and solutions that will revolutionise the industry, improve rural residents' quality of life, and release the sector's full potential. By acknowledging the importance of these problems, we move closer to a vision in which agriculture in Afghanistan thrives, rural communities prosper, and the country's economy is revitalised and stabilised.

5.2- Discuss the socioeconomic impact of these challenges on rural communities.

A Struggle for Survival: The Social and Economic Impacts on Rural Areas

Introduction

The difficulties that Afghan farmers encounter, as discussed in the preceding chapter, are not separate problems but rather integral parts of the economic and social fabric of rural areas. The effects of these difficulties on the lives and livelihoods of rural Afghans are explored in this chapter. Each problem—from the persistent deterioration of fertile soil to the lack of access to modern technology, from the dearth of water for irrigation to the ever-present threat of pests and diseases—reverberates through the economic and social fabric of rural Afghanistan. The Afghan people's endurance and ingenuity are shown in this chapter as the author untangles the intricate web of relationships between threats and rural villages.

Degradation of land leading to loss of livelihoods is discussed in Section 8.1.

The socioeconomic consequences of land degradation, such as soil erosion, salinization, and desertification, are particularly felt in rural areas. In this article, we look at how declining farmland threatens our ability to feed ourselves. We look at how land degradation affects farmers' incomes and safety, and how that impacts society as a whole. We also stress the importance of sustainable land management practises for revitalising degraded land and improving rural communities.

Part 8.2: The Digital Divide and the Problem of Slow Adoption of New Technologies

Farmers' economic prospects are hampered by the widespread lack of adoption of contemporary technology in rural areas. Here, we look into the obstacles that farmers encounter while trying to acquire and employ technology. We investigate how the information gap prevents people from gaining skills and accessing markets, thereby limiting their ability to make a living. We also highlight the potential of technology adoption to strengthen rural communities and their ability to make a living.

Section 8.3: Irrigation Difficulties - Hungry for Progress

Socioeconomic situations in rural areas are impacted by inefficient irrigation systems caused by a lack of water and inadequate infrastructure. We examine the difficulties of farming and livestock raising in areas with scarce water supplies. We examine how low irrigation rates affect agricultural revenue and food security, highlighting the precarious position of rural populations. We also highlight the importance of better irrigation systems in increasing agricultural output, expanding economic opportunities, and decreasing poverty.

Section 8.4: Dangerous Pests and Diseases that Threaten Economic Security

Crops are constantly at risk from pests and diseases, diminishing rural areas' economic potential. Here, we look into the connection between the spread of pests and illnesses in farming and the ensuing loss of productivity and rise in input costs. We examine the monetary effects, paying special attention to the potential for food insecurity and falling revenues among farmers. We also stress the significance of pest and disease management in protecting rural economies and bolstering resilience.

Economic Inequality: The Gap Widens (Section 8.5)

Rural growth is hindered by economic inequality, which exists both within and across farming communities. Here, we examine the effects of farmers' unequal access to resources, markets, and financing on their economic and social standing. We look at the difficulties encountered by smallholder farmers and underprivileged communities, with special focus on their restricted access to economic resources. We also stress the importance of policies that are not exclusive and which work to increase economic fairness and the influence of all members of the agricultural community.

Survival Threatened by Uncertainty and War (Section 8.6)

Rural Afghans' socioeconomic conditions are negatively impacted by the long and ominous shadow of insecurity and violence. Security threats, such as landmines, rebel attacks, and population displacement, are discussed in this section. In this article, we take a look at how agricultural productivity and economic stability suffer when people are afraid to farm or own property. We also highlight the importance of initiatives that protect rural populations from the effects of insecurity and war.

Climate change: how to deal with the unknown

Due to climate change, rural areas may experience more frequent and severe weather occurrences. Here, we go into the research on how global warming influences farming methods, water availability, and food safety. We investigate crop failure, decreased revenues, and heightened vulnerability as social and economic effects of climate-related shocks. To further strengthen resistance to climate change, protect rural livelihoods, and guarantee the long-term viability of rural communities, we stress the significance of adaption techniques.

Conclusion

This section sheds light on the complex relationship between the difficulties Afghan farmers experience and the economic and social climate in rural areas. The lives and livelihoods of rural Afghans are shaped by factors such as land degradation, low technology adoption, irrigation difficulties, pests and diseases, economic inequality, insecurity and violence, and climate change. This is a fight for survival, and it exemplifies the tenacity, ingenuity, and dedication to place that define a people. While recognising the resiliency of Afghan farmers in the face of these difficulties, we must equally accept the critical need for ideas and actions that improve their economic prospects, increase their living conditions, and safeguard their future. This shows the resilience of rural areas, which are the backbone of Afghan agriculture and the source of the country's future prosperity and stability.

Chapter 6:
Building Up the System

6.1- Detail the importance of infrastructure development, particularly in transportation and storage facilities.

Infrastructure growth is the bedrock of agricultural advancement, as discussed in Chapter 9.

Introduction

In a country like Afghanistan, where inhospitable terrain and a turbulent history have hindered communication and the distribution of resources, infrastructure development is crucial to agricultural advancement. In this section, we discuss the significance of developing infrastructure, particularly transport and storage centres. These infrastructures serve as not just pathways for development but also catalysts for rural revitalization and commercial expansion. We discover the transformative potential of infrastructure development in Afghanistan's agricultural sector by analysing their function in expanding access to markets, decreasing post-harvest losses, and encouraging agribusiness.

Transportation Networks: Linking Production Areas to Consumer Markets

Connecting agricultural production areas to local and global markets is impossible without a reliable and well-maintained transportation network. This section examines the difficulties caused by Afghanistan's insufficient road infrastructure. We look at how rural areas' lack of investment in transport causes them to be shut out of economic opportunities and to face higher transaction costs and fewer customers. We also emphasise the transformative power of infrastructure investments like new roads, bridges, and transportation networks to open up previously unreachable markets, ease trade barriers, and stimulate economic development.

Subsection 9.1.1: Road Building: Creating Opportunities for Success.

Building roads connects farmers with urban consumers, making them an essential part of every transport infrastructure project.
Inadequate road networks and their implications for rural populations are explored in this section. Specifically, we examine how all-weather roads might help farmers save money on transportation, get easier access to markets, and expand their export potential.

Section 9.1.2: Bridge Construction – Overcoming Obstacles

Bridges are crucial parts of the transportation network, especially in a country with a varied landscape. This section explores the difficulties caused by Afghanistan's deficient bridge network. We examine how bridge defects affect the economy, focusing on how they cut off towns from one another and make it harder for people to go to and from marketplaces. We also highlight the importance of bridge building in promoting economic growth, accessibility, and communication between rural areas.

Storage Facilities for Maintaining the Harvest is discussed in Section 9.2.

For agricultural products to maintain their quality and quantity after harvest, with minimal post-harvest losses, storage facilities are essential. In this article, we examine the problems caused by Afghanistan's rudimentary storage facilities. We take a look at how farmers, consumers, and the overall food system are impacted when cold storage options are limited. We also highlight the revolutionary potential of storage facilities, such as cold storage units and warehouses, to increase the viability of agricultural products over time, reduce waste, and improve access to nutritious food.

Section 9.2.1: Refrigerated Warehouses for Prolonged Storage

Preserving the quality and freshness of perishable agricultural goods requires the use of cold storage facilities. In this part, we discuss some of the difficulties caused by the lack of refrigeration infrastructure in Afghanistan. Post-harvest losses, decreased income for farmers, and restricted access to markets are discussed as a result of a lack of cold storage facilities. We also emphasise the economic advantages of cold storage facilities, including their function in prolonging the shelf life of fruits, vegetables, and other perishable commodities, decreasing food waste, and guaranteeing a constant supply of fresh produce.

Storage Facilities: a Safety Valve Against Market Swings

Food security may be maintained and the effects of market fluctuations can be mitigated thanks to the availability of agricultural products stored in warehouses. In this section, we delve into the difficulties caused by Afghanistan's undeveloped warehousing facilities. We discuss how unstable food prices and a lack of storage space for crops result from a lack of warehouses. Furthermore, we emphasise the monetary benefits of warehouse facilities, such as their function in regulating pricing, decreasing post-harvest losses, and expanding farmers' access to markets.

Market Facilitation for Agricultural Enterprises 9.3

The expansion of agribusiness and the selling of agricultural products relies heavily on the availability of adequate market facilities. In this article, we examine the obstacles presented by Afghanistan's antiquated market infrastructure. We take a look at how insufficient market infrastructure impedes value addition, prevents farmers from reaching high-value customers, and stunts the growth of the agricultural sector. We also emphasise the transformative potential of market infrastructure, such as wholesale markets and processing centres, in improving the value chain, increasing market penetration, and promoting economic growth.

Agribusiness Centres in Wholesale Markets (Section 9.3.1)

To aggregate and distribute agricultural produce, wholesale markets act as nodes for agribusiness. This section explores the difficulties caused by Afghanistan's dearth of wholesale markets. We look at how the lack of wholesale markets hinders price discovery, lessens market transparency, and gives farmers less leverage in negotiations. We also highlight the importance of wholesale markets from an economic perspective, highlighting its function in facilitating farmers' access to higher-value markets, increasing price competitiveness, and promoting agribusiness growth.

To add value to agricultural products, see Section 9.3.2 on Processing Centres.

Agricultural products gain in value and farmers get access to new revenue streams thanks in large part to central processing facilities. In this part, we examine the difficulties caused by Afghanistan's dearth of processing hubs. We

 Determine how the limited capacity to add value to agricultural products due to a lack of processing facilities has a negative impact on farmers' income. We also emphasise the monetary benefits of processing centres, including how they improve agricultural product quality, open up new markets for processed goods, and encourage the expansion of the agribusiness sector.

Conclusion

This section emphasises the significance of improving Afghanistan's transportation and storage facilities in reshaping the country's agricultural industry. Building roads and bridges connects more people to more markets at lower cost, which in turn boosts consumer spending and the economy. Cold storage units and warehouses are two examples of storage facilities that help ensure that food is not wasted after harvest. Buildings like wholesale markets and processing centres help farmers gain access to more lucrative markets and increase the value of their products. A stronger agricultural sector that helps rural areas, gives farmers more control over their lives, and boosts the economy is possible thanks to the recognition of the transformative power of infrastructure development.

6.2- Discuss ongoing and potential infrastructure projects aimed at improving the agricultural sector.

Infrastructure growth is the bedrock of agricultural advancement, as discussed in Chapter 9.

Introduction

In a country like Afghanistan, where inhospitable terrain and a turbulent history have hindered communication and the distribution of resources, infrastructure development is crucial to agricultural advancement. In this section, we discuss the significance of developing infrastructure, particularly transport and storage centres. These infrastructures serve as not just pathways for development but also catalysts for rural revitalization and commercial expansion. We discover the transformative potential of infrastructure development in Afghanistan's agricultural sector by analysing their function in expanding access to markets, decreasing post-harvest losses, and encouraging agribusiness.

Transportation Networks: Linking Production Areas to Consumer Markets

Connecting agricultural production areas to local and global markets is impossible without a reliable and well-maintained transportation network. This section examines the difficulties caused by Afghanistan's insufficient road infrastructure. We look at how rural areas' lack of investment in transport causes them to be shut out of economic opportunities and to face higher transaction costs and fewer customers. We also emphasise the transformative power of infrastructure investments like new roads, bridges, and transportation networks to open up previously unreachable markets, ease trade barriers, and stimulate economic development.

Subsection 9.1.1: Road Building: Creating Opportunities for Success.

Building roads connects farmers with urban consumers, making them an essential part of every transport infrastructure project. Inadequate road networks and their implications for rural populations are explored in this section. Specifically, we examine how all-weather roads might help farmers save money on transportation, get easier access to markets, and expand their export potential.

Section 9.1.2: Bridge Construction – Overcoming Obstacles

Bridges are crucial parts of the transportation network, especially in a country with a varied landscape. This section explores the difficulties caused by Afghanistan's deficient bridge network. We examine how bridge defects affect the economy, focusing on how they cut off towns from one another and make it harder for people to go to and from marketplaces. We also highlight the importance of bridge building in promoting economic growth, accessibility, and communication between rural areas.

Storage Facilities for Maintaining the Harvest is discussed in Section 9.2.

For agricultural products to maintain their quality and quantity after harvest, with minimal post-harvest losses, storage facilities are essential. In this article, we examine the problems caused by Afghanistan's rudimentary storage facilities. We take a look at how farmers, consumers, and the overall food system are impacted when cold storage options are limited. We also highlight the revolutionary potential of storage facilities, such as cold storage units and warehouses, to increase the viability of agricultural products over time, reduce waste, and improve access to nutritious food.

Section 9.2.1: Refrigerated Warehouses for Prolonged Storage

Preserving the quality and freshness of perishable agricultural goods requires the use of cold storage facilities. In this part, we discuss some of the difficulties caused by the lack of refrigeration infrastructure in Afghanistan. Post-harvest losses, decreased income for farmers, and restricted access to markets are discussed as a result of a lack of cold storage facilities. We also emphasise the economic advantages of cold storage facilities, including their function in prolonging the shelf life of fruits, vegetables, and other perishable commodities, decreasing food waste, and guaranteeing a constant supply of fresh produce.

Storage Facilities: a Safety Valve Against Market Swings

Food security may be maintained and the effects of market fluctuations can be mitigated thanks to the availability of agricultural products stored in warehouses. In this section, we delve into the difficulties caused by Afghanistan's undeveloped warehousing facilities. We discuss how unstable food prices and a lack of storage space for crops result from a lack of warehouses. Furthermore, we emphasise the monetary benefits of warehouse facilities, such as their function in regulating pricing, decreasing post-harvest losses, and expanding farmers' access to markets.

Market Facilitation for Agricultural Enterprises 9.3

The expansion of agribusiness and the selling of agricultural products relies heavily on the availability of adequate market facilities. In this article, we examine the obstacles presented by Afghanistan's antiquated market infrastructure. We take a look at how insufficient market infrastructure impedes value addition, prevents farmers from reaching high-value customers, and stunts the growth of the agricultural sector. We also emphasise the transformative potential of market infrastructure, such as wholesale markets and processing centres, in improving the value chain, increasing market penetration, and promoting economic growth.

Agribusiness Centres in Wholesale Markets (Section 9.3.1)

To aggregate and distribute agricultural produce, wholesale markets act as nodes for agribusiness. This section explores the difficulties caused by Afghanistan's dearth of wholesale markets. We look at how the lack of wholesale markets hinders price discovery, lessens market transparency, and gives farmers less leverage in negotiations. We also highlight the importance of wholesale markets from an economic perspective, highlighting its function in facilitating farmers' access to higher-value markets, increasing price competitiveness, and promoting agribusiness growth.

To add value to agricultural products, see Section 9.3.2 on Processing Centres.

Agricultural products gain in value and farmers get access to new revenue streams thanks in large part to central processing facilities. In this part, we examine the difficulties caused by Afghanistan's dearth of processing hubs. We

Determine how the limited capacity to add value to agricultural products due to a lack of processing facilities has a negative impact on farmers' income. We also emphasise the monetary benefits of processing centres, including how they improve agricultural product quality, open up new markets for processed goods, and encourage the expansion of the agribusiness sector.

Conclusion

This section emphasises the significance of improving Afghanistan's transportation and storage facilities in reshaping the country's agricultural industry. Building roads and bridges connects more people to more markets at lower cost, which in turn boosts consumer spending and the economy. Cold storage units and warehouses are two examples of storage facilities that help ensure that food is not wasted after harvest. Buildings like wholesale markets and processing centres help farmers gain access to more lucrative markets and increase the value of their products. A stronger agricultural sector that helps rural areas, gives farmers more control over their lives, and boosts the economy is possible thanks to the recognition of the transformative power of infrastructure development.

Chapter 7:
Sustainability through Water Resource Management

7.1- Examine the need for efficient water management in Afghanistan's agriculture.

The Roots of Prosperity: Effective Water Management in Afghan Agriculture

Introduction

As water is a limited and valuable resource in Afghanistan, effective water management is of critical importance to the country's agricultural sector. Recognising the importance of water in sustaining the foundation of a prosperous society, this chapter delves into the topic of water management in Afghanistan's agricultural sector. We investigate how sustainable water management practises can revolutionise agriculture in Afghanistan in the face of water scarcity and the negative effects of ineffective irrigation. We offer light on the way to resilience, productivity, and prosperity for Afghan farmers by analysing policies and programmes focused at optimising water use.

Ahead, we face the formidable obstacle of water scarcity (Section 11.1).

Afghanistan's agricultural output and food security are both threatened by a lack of available water. This section explores the severity of water scarcity across the country, focusing on its effect on rural areas and the agricultural economy. We take a look at the ways in which water scarcity impacts agriculture, livestock, and exposure to climate change. In addition, we stress the significance of developing plans to alleviate water scarcity and secure a steady flow of water for agricultural use.

The Helmand River Basin is a source of concern (Section 11.1.1).

Extreme water scarcity has reached crisis proportions in the Helmand River Basin of Afghanistan. The importance of the Helmand River Basin, the difficulties in managing its water supply, and the effects on agricultural communities are discussed in this section. We take a look at the effects of water shortage in this watershed on farming, irrigation methods, and people's ability to make a living in the countryside. The need of sustainable water management in securing a reliable supply of water for agriculture in the Helmand River Basin is also emphasised.

The Kabul River Basin: Quenching Sustainability (Section 11.1.2)

The Kabul River Basin is experiencing a similar water shortage that is having an effect on farming and cities. The significance of the Kabul River Basin, the difficulties in managing its water supply, and the effects on both rural and urban areas are discussed in this section. We investigate the impacts on agriculture, water quality, and city sustainability caused by water scarcity in this watershed. To combat water scarcity and promote agricultural and urban sustainability in the Kabul River Basin, we also emphasise the importance of sustainable water management.

Section 11.2: Wasteful Irrigation Wastes Money.

Afghanistan's agricultural output suffers from inefficient irrigation methods that make water scarcity problems even worse. We look at water loss, soil deterioration, and higher production costs as results of poor irrigation systems. In this article, we'll look at how conventional irrigation practises restrict harvests, waste water, and slow agricultural progress. We also stress the significance of efficient and environmentally friendly irrigation methods to boost agricultural output.

Traditional furrow irrigation has a long history of inefficiency, as discussed in Section 11.2.1.

Common but inefficient, traditional furrow irrigation causes water loss and soil damage in Afghanistan. This section delves into the history of furrow irrigation, how it affects farmers' water consumption, and the difficulties it creates for rural populations. The effects of this technique on agricultural yields, water use, and soil erosion are analysed. We also stress the importance of upgrading to more effective irrigation methods to reduce water waste and boost crop production.

Drip irrigation is discussed in Section 11.2.2 as a cutting-edge technique.

Drip irrigation is a cutting-edge method that minimises wasteful watering of crops. Drip irrigation is discussed below, along with its potential water-saving qualities and the advantages it provides to farmers. We take a look at how drip irrigation increases crop yields while decreasing water waste and increasing water usage efficiency. We also stress the value of encouraging the widespread use of drip irrigation as a method of water conservation in Afghan farming.

A Roadmap to Water Sustainability and Resilience (Section 11.3)

In order to alleviate water scarcity and strengthen Afghan agriculture's resilience, sustainable water management practises are essential. This section explores the policies and programmes that are working to improve water management in the long-term. We look at their role in reducing water consumption, boosting crop yields, and securing food supplies. We also emphasise the transformative potential of these practises in bolstering the economic and physical security of Afghan farmers.

Capturing Excess Water Through Water Harvesting Methods 11.3.1

In dry locations, rainwater is a scarce resource that must be captured and stored using water harvesting techniques. In this section, we'll discuss the relevance of water harvesting, how it can affect water availability, and what advantages it can bring to rural communities and their farmers. We take a look at how water collection helps restore aquifers, boosts moisture levels in the soil, and makes crops more resistant to drought. Water harvesting as a method of long-term water management is also emphasised as crucial for Afghanistan.

Aquifer Recharging: Reestablishing Water Levels

Recharging aquifers is an essential method for bringing groundwater levels back into equilibrium. In this part, we discuss the role of aquifer recharge in restocking aquifers and the advantages it provides to agricultural production. We take a look at how aquifer recharge improves crop yields by raising the amount of water available for irrigation. We also stress the significance of aquifer recharging as a method of long-term water management in Afghanistan.

Community-based water management that increases farmer agency is discussed in Section 11.3.3.

Farmers are given the tools they need to effectively manage and distribute available water through community-based water management programmes. In this section, we discuss the value of community-based water management, its effects on water distribution, and the advantages it provides to agricultural communities. We look at how these programmes improve water allocation, lessen water wars, and boost agricultural output. Furthermore, we stress the significance of community-based water management as a long-term practise that strengthens agricultural resilience in Afghanistan by giving authority back to farmers.

Conclusion

The importance of water management in agriculture in Afghanistan is emphasised in this chapter. Challenges to agricultural production and food security arise from water constraint, ineffective irrigation, and unsustainable water practises. We foresee a future where Afghan agriculture may flourish even in desert regions by recognising the value of sustainable water management practises including water harvesting, aquifer recharge, and community-based water management. These methods not only help Afghan farmers cope with the difficulties they face, but they also open the path for increased productivity and economic growth for the entire country. To ensure a long-lasting and prosperous agricultural industry in Afghanistan, proper water management is essential.

7.2- Discuss the impact of climate change on water resources and propose sustainable solutions.

Impact of Climate Change on Water Resources and Long-Term Solutions (Chapter 12).

Introduction

Global ecosystems, human communities, and economy are all threatened by climate change. The repercussions of climate change are most noticeable in Afghanistan, a country that is already struggling with water scarcity and resource management challenges. This chapter examines how changes in precipitation patterns, glacier melting, and the frequency of extreme weather events are having a substantial impact on Afghanistan's water supplies. To further protect the nation's water resources and guarantee a more sustainable future, it also investigates sustainable alternatives such as adaption techniques and resilient water management practises.

Altering precipitation patterns: a conundrum for water supplies

In Afghanistan, the paradox of changing precipitation patterns brought on by global warming is already being felt. This section looks at how climate change has caused the region to experience both droughts and floods due to changes in the normal patterns of precipitation. The effects of these shifts on water supply, soil moisture, and agricultural practises are investigated. It also highlights the importance of adopting adaptive water management practises to meet the problems brought on by varying rainfall.

Droughts - The Parched Landscapes, Section 12.1.1.

Changing patterns of precipitation have caused droughts in Afghanistan to become increasingly often and severe. This section examines why droughts matter, how they affect water supplies, and how they affect farming and rural people. The effects of extended droughts on water supply, soil moisture, and crop yields are investigated. Drought-resistant agricultural types, water conservation, and efficient irrigation are also highlighted as crucial measures for reducing the negative effects of droughts.

Floods: The Deluge Catch-22 is discussed in Section 12.1.2.

While changes in precipitation patterns might amplify the effects of floods, they only represent one side of the water resource paradox in Afghanistan. In this section, we'll talk about how important floods are, how they affect water supplies, and how they affect farming and rural areas. The effects of flooding, both flash and river, on soil, water, and crops are analysed. It also highlights the need for flood prevention measures including better water drainage, early warning systems, and flood-resistant crop varieties.

Section 12.2: Glacier Melt, a Threat to Water Supply

A noticeable and disturbing effect of global warming is the melting of glaciers in the Hindu Kush-Himalaya region. This section looks at the dangers to water quality and availability caused by the melting of glaciers in the region, particularly Afghanistan. It investigates how glacial melt affects river flow, soil moisture, and agricultural sustainability. It also highlights the importance of adaptive techniques like monitoring glaciers and making good use of glacier-fed streams to deal with the problems that may arise when glaciers melt.

Glacial meltwater is an essential resource, as discussed in Section 12.2.1.

In the high alpine regions of Afghanistan, glacial meltwater provides an essential water resource. In this section, we will examine the relevance of glacier meltwater, including its effect on river flow and its importance to agricultural sustainability. It looks at the role of glacier meltwater in sustaining agriculture at high altitudes by means of irrigation, soil moisture, and crop production. It also highlights the significance of sustainable practises that save glacial water and efficient methods of utilising this precious resource.

Increasing Worries About River Flow Variability, Section 12.2.2

River flow variability is a major concern for water resource management in Afghanistan due to its influence from glacial melt and shifting precipitation patterns. The relevance of river flow fluctuation, its effect on water availability, and the repercussions for agriculture are discussed in this section. The effects of river flow variability on irrigation consistency, soil moisture, and crop yields are analysed. It also emphasises the need for water management practises that are flexible enough to accommodate these shifts and guarantee a consistent water supply for farming.

Extreme weather events and unforeseen disasters are discussed in Section 12.3.

Climate change is increasing the frequency and unpredictability of extreme weather events including storms, heatwaves, and cold snaps. The effects of severe weather on Afghanistan's water supply are discussed in this section. Topics covered include infrastructure damage, water contamination, and agricultural disturbance. It delves into why adaptive strategies and resilient water management are necessary to lessen the blow of climate change.

Random Catastrophes 12.3.1 Severe Weather and Flooding

Flooding, landslides, and damaged infrastructure are all possible outcomes of the intense storms and rain that are commonly connected with climate change. This section discusses the importance of storms and strong rainfall, how they affect water supplies, and how they affect farming. It delves into the ways in which these calamities wreck irrigation networks, taint water supplies, and ruin harvests. It also highlights the need for disaster planning, flood prevention, and infrastructure that can withstand the pressures of extreme weather.

Section 12.3.2: Extreme Temperatures, Such as Heat Waves and Cold Snaps

Extreme weather, such as heatwaves and cold snaps, can have a negative impact on agriculture and water supplies. This section delves into the relevance of severe temperatures, how they affect water availability, and the results for agriculture and cattle. The effects of heatwaves on water evaporation and soil moisture, as well as the effects of cold snaps on frozen water supplies and crop damage, are investigated. To lessen the blow of temperature swings, it also highlights the value of water-saving measures, effective irrigation, and flexible farming techniques.

Sustainable Solutions for a Changing Climate is discussed in Section 12.4.

Resilient responses are crucial for coping with

climate change and protecting Afghanistan's water supply. In this section, we'll look at several different approaches to water management and adaptive measures for coping with climate change. Effective irrigation, drought-resistant crop cultivation, water conservation, glacier observation, flood prevention strategies, and robust infrastructure are all discussed. It also stresses the importance of policy backing, community involvement, and international cooperation in bolstering Afghan agriculture's resilience and assuring a more secure and sustainable future.

Optimising Water Use in Irrigation Systems (Section 12.4.1)

To maximise water consumption in a warming climate, efficient irrigation practises, such as drip irrigation and water-saving measures, are essential. In this section, we'll examine how efficient irrigation helps farmers save water and what other advantages it provides. In this article, we'll look at how these techniques can boost agricultural yields while decreasing water waste. It also highlights the need to promote and adopt efficient irrigation technologies to deal with the difficulties brought on by shifting rainfall patterns and water scarcity.

Adapting Drought-Resistant Crops to Limited Water Supplies, Section 12.4.2

When dealing with water shortages and shifting rainfall patterns, having access to drought-resistant crop cultivars is crucial. In this section, we'll talk about the value of drought-resistant crops, how they affect overall agricultural resilience, and what kinds of advantages they bring to farmers. The article investigates the drought resistance, improved crop yields, and reduced negative effects of different plant types. It also emphasises the need to produce and promote drought-resistant crops to boost agricultural output in a warming world.

Water conservation is discussed in Section 12.4.3, "Conserving a Valuable Resource."

Rainwater harvesting and other forms of soil moisture management are essential to sustaining Afghanistan's water supply. This section discusses why water conservation is so important, how it affects water supply, and how it helps those living in rural areas. It delves into the ways that water conservation helps restore aquifers, boosts soil moisture, and strengthens crop resistance. More than that, it highlights the significance of promoting and adopting water conservation practises as part of sustainable water management in Afghan agriculture.

Glaciers are a dynamic resource that must be monitored over time.

In the Hindu Kush-Himalaya region, monitoring glaciers is essential for keeping tabs on glacier melt and river flow fluctuations. The importance of glacier monitoring, its effect on water resource management, and the advantages it provides to agriculture are discussed in this section. It looks at how monitoring glaciers can help with things like water distribution, irrigation strategy, and flood prevention. It also shows how monitoring glaciers may help us adjust to the difficulties faced by things like glacial melt and erratic river flows.

Subsection 12.4.5: Flood Prevention and Risk Reduction

The dangers associated with extreme weather can be reduced by the implementation of flood control measures such as early warning systems and robust infrastructure. This section discusses the importance of flood management measures, how they affect disaster preparedness, and how they assist rural areas. The article delves into the ways in which these safeguards help prevent floods, preserve water supplies, and guarantee agricultural stability. It also highlights the significance of flood control measures in the context of climate resilience initiatives in Afghan agriculture.

Conclusion

This chapter emphasises the importance of finding long-term solutions to the problem of climate change's devastating effects on Afghanistan's water supply. Extreme weather, glacial melting, and shifting rainfall patterns all pose serious threats to water supply and quality. We foresee a future where agriculture in Afghanistan may flourish despite a changing environment by implementing adaptable methods and water management practises. These measures not only lessen the destructive effects of global warming, but also open the path for increased toughness, output, and longevity. By adopting these environmentally responsible policies, Afghanistan will be able to protect its water supply for the benefit of future generations of farmers and rural residents.

Chapter 8:
Promotion of Agricultural Knowledge and Technology Transfer

8.1- Explore the role of agricultural education and extension services in improving farmers' knowledge and skills.

Chapter 13: Providing Agricultural Education and Extension Services to Improve the Lives of Afghan Farmers.

Introduction

Agricultural education and extension services are crucial in Afghanistan since agriculture is the backbone of the economy and provides a living for millions of people. This chapter explores the many ways in which education and extension play a pivotal role in helping farmers increase agricultural output, adjust to new circumstances, and boost their personal and financial well-being. We examine how education and extension services provide essential tools to farmers, encourage the spread of cutting-edge technology, foster the adoption of environmentally friendly methods, and advance agriculture in Afghanistan.

Agricultural Education: Building a Solid Foundation

The education farmers receive in Afghanistan is crucial to their success. Education in agriculture, both formally at colleges and universities and informally in farmer field schools, is discussed here. Here, we investigate the ways in which farmers might benefit from improved access to information and knowledge through educational opportunities. We also stress the need to improve and broaden agricultural education programmes in Afghanistan to provide farmers with the skills they'll need to make their farms sustainable and lucrative.

Agricultural Colleges and Universities: Developing Future Farmers and Ranchers

The training of agricultural experts and professionals relies heavily on educational institutions dedicated to the field. In this section, we examine the role of universities in the advancement of agriculture in Afghanistan, focusing on the significance of agricultural universities and the programmes they offer. We examine how these schools provide tailored education, perform important research, and equip their graduates to meet the specific needs of Afghan farmers. To satisfy the expanding need for agricultural skills in the country, we also emphasise the importance of investing in agricultural universities.

Subsection 13.1.2: Agricultural Vocational Education and Skill Improvement.

Farmers in Afghanistan benefit from vocational training programmes because of the information and expertise they impart. The value of vocational education, its curriculum, and its effects on skill acquisition are discussed here. We look at how these courses improve farmers' technical skills through instruction in current farming methods and hands-on practise. We also stress the significance of increasing access to vocational education, particularly in rural regions, in order to provide farmers with the tools they need to practise environmentally responsible farming.

Learn by doing on the farm with "Subsection 13.1.3: Farmer Field Schools."

Farmer field schools encourage active learning via hands-on experience in agriculture. This section discusses the value of farmer field schools, the approaches they take, and the results they achieve in terms of information exchange. We investigate how these institutions facilitate learning through direct farmer participation, foster information sharing among farmers, and inspire farmers to embrace environmentally friendly methods of farming. We also highlight the promise of farmer field schools as a means of distributing useful and locally relevant agricultural information to farmers in Afghanistan.

Knowledge at Your Fingertips: Extension Services Section 13.2

The agricultural support systems in Afghanistan would not function without extension services. The value of agricultural extension, which includes public and private initiatives, trial fields, and consultation services, is discussed below. We look at how extension services deliver information and tools to farmers, allowing them to better manage their crops, eliminate pests, and make the most of their available resources. To fill the information gap and strengthen farmers' abilities, we also stress the significance of extending and enhancing extension programmes.

Government programmes with a national scope are discussed in Section 13.2.1.

There is a widespread reach for Afghanistan's government-led extension programmes. In this section, we examine the role of government extension services, how they are organised, and the effect they have on rural areas. We look into how these initiatives train farmers around the country and spread agricultural knowledge. We also stress the importance of governmental extension services in advancing agriculture and enhancing farmers' incomes.

Non-Governmental Organisations (NGOs) - Multiple Perspectives (Section 13.2.2)

In Afghanistan, agricultural extension is provided through a wide range of non-governmental organisations (NGOs). This section delves into the role of NGOs in delivering extension services, the methods they use, and the effect this has on spreading information. We look at how these groups interact with farmers, provide regionally relevant services, and advocate for environmentally responsible methods of agriculture. We also highlight the potential of NGO-led extension services in meeting the specific requirements of different communities and regions in Afghanistan.

Section 13.2.3: Demonstration Plots - Experience-Based Education

Farmers can learn a lot from visiting demonstration plots. This section discusses the value of demonstration plots, why they're used, and how they aid in skill acquisition. We discuss the role that demonstration plots have in educating farmers about new techniques, tools, and crop types through direct exposure and experimentation. We also stress the need for more demonstration plots to be used to teach Afghan farmers about sustainable and cutting-edge farming practises.

Transitioning Information and Experience: Section 13.3

The foundation of agricultural education and extension in Afghanistan is the sharing of knowledge. Radio shows, mobile devices, and local networks are just a few of the knowledge dissemination mediums that are dissected in this section. We investigate how these lines of contact fill the informational void, extend to underserved areas, and give farmers the tools they need to make educated decisions. We also highlight the role that new forms of communication could have in reshaping agriculture in Afghanistan.

The Voice of Agriculture Radio Programmes (13.3.1)

To reach farmers in rural areas that are difficult to access, radio programmes are an effective medium. In this section, we examine the role of radio broadcasts in the diffusion of information and the significance of the programmes they air. We look at how these programmes help farmers by providing them with data on crop management, weather forecasts, and market prices. We also emphasise the value of radio programmes for reaching farmers who have few other options for obtaining agricultural knowledge.

Mobile technology and the digital revolution are discussed in Section 13.3.2.

In Afghanistan, the dissemination of agricultural information through mobile technologies is experiencing rapid growth. In this section, we discuss the relevance of mobile technology, its uses, and the effects it has on the availability of information. We look at how farmers' access to real-time information, training resources, and expert guidance through mobile apps, SMS services, and voice messaging helps them make better decisions. We also highlight the importance of mobile technology's ability to increase farmers' access to information and spark a digital revolution in Afghanistan's agricultural sector.

Community-Based Networks for Peer-to-Peer Learning

The ability to share information and experiences among farmers is greatly facilitated through community networks. This section delves into the function, structure, and effect of community networks on informal education. We investigate how these systems bring farmers together, encourage the spread of information, and encourage the use of environmentally friendly methods. We also highlight the potential of community networks in fostering a sense of belonging and solidarity among Afghan farmers, thereby facilitating their ability to cooperatively address agricultural difficulties and opportunities.

Sustainability and Resilience: Constructing Afghanistan's Agricultural Future

The sustainability and resilience of Afghan agriculture are greatly aided by agricultural education and extension programmes. In this article, we discuss how education and extension may help the agricultural industry become more sustainable and resilient. We look at how these services equip farmers to deal with climate change and other difficulties. We also stress the need for sustained funding and governmental backing to bolster the influence of education and extension on agriculture's trajectory in Afghanistan.

Sustainable Methods for Building Resilience (Section 13.4.1)

Resilience in Afghan farming is best built through the use of sustainable agricultural practises. The importance of sustainable practises, their effect on resource conservation, and the advantages they provide to farmers are discussed in this section. We discuss how these methods strengthen agricultural resilience to climate change by improving soil quality, optimising water use, and decreasing environmental impact. To further strengthen agriculture in Afghanistan for the long term, we stress the value of incorporating sustainable practises into agricultural education and extension activities.

Adaptation to Climate Change: Manoeuvring Uncertainty (Section 13.4.2)

Afghan agriculture must adapt to climate change if it is to become more resilient. This section delves into the relevance of climate change adaptation, the tactics used to adapt, and the results for farmers. We look at how agricultural education and extension may explain adaptive methods that help farmers adjust to new environments, reduce vulnerability, and safeguard their incomes. We also stress the significance of incorporating climate change adaptation into educational and extension programmes to equip farmers with the knowledge and skills they'll need to face the future with confidence.

Subsection 13.4.3: Policy Assistance in Fostering Educational and Extension Programmes

Policy backing is crucial for the development and improvement of Afghanistan's agricultural education and extension services. In this section, we discuss the importance of supportive policies, how they affect the agricultural industry, and how they help increase access to education and extension. Here, we investigate the potential of policy interventions to increase access to education and extension services for underserved populations, encourage investment, and boost service quality. We also stress the need of policy dedication to aid in the advancement of agriculture in Afghanistan via educational outreach programmes.

Conclusion

The importance of agricultural education and extension services in equipping Afghan farmers with the skills necessary for productive and environmentally friendly farming is emphasised in this chapter. Farmers gain access to cutting-edge methods and practises through education, be it at a classroom or in the field. Through government and non-government programmes, extension services bring information to even the most rural farms. Farmers in Afghanistan are given more access to information and better tools for decision-making thanks to novel approaches like mobile technology and community networks.

These services also aid in the adoption of sustainable practises and adaption to climate change in Afghanistan's agricultural sector. The future of agriculture in Afghanistan is bright as policy support increases the importance of education and extension. A more prosperous and resilient agricultural sector will improve the lives of millions of Afghan farmers and contribute to the country's economic growth and food security if we invest in the education and training of those farmers now.

8.2- Highlight the potential of modern agricultural technologies in increasing productivity.

Chapter 14: "Modern Agricultural Technologies as a Catalyst for Boosting Afghan Agricultural Productivity"

Introduction

Modern agricultural technologies offer Afghanistan a glimmer of optimism, with the potential to transform farming methods, boost output, and fuel economic growth. This section explores how new agricultural technologies could serve as a catalyst for boosting agricultural output in Afghanistan. From precision farming and mechanisation to biotechnology and digital solutions, we look at how these developments can help farmers increase their harvests while decreasing their input costs and enhancing their quality of life.

Precision farming, or precision horticulture, is discussed in Section 14.1.

Precision farming is a fundamental component of contemporary agriculture, providing Afghan farmers with the tools they need to more precisely and efficiently cultivate their land. The importance of precision farming, its components, and its effect on crop yields are discussed here. In this article, we'll look at how GPS, drones, and data analytics help farmers get their planting, watering, and pest control just so. Further, we stress the promise of precision farming in minimising waste, cutting expenses, and maximising harvests.

GPS Technology: A Roadmap for Accuracy, Section 14.1.1

Precision farming relies heavily on Global Positioning System (GPS) technology, which facilitates accurate field planning and management. Here we discuss the role of global positioning system (GPS) technology and its implications for farming. We investigate how GPS helps with precise land mapping, mechanised control, and directional fieldwork. We also note the promise of global positioning system (GPS) technology in helping farmers in Afghanistan improve their techniques and output.

Subsection 14.1.2: UAVs: Precise Views from Above

In precision farming, drones act as aerial scouts, gathering crucial information for farmers. This section discusses the relevance of drones, the scope of their skills, and the effects they have on agricultural management. We take a look at how drones help farmers by taking aerial photos, checking on their crops, and locating any problems so they can fix them quickly and efficiently. We also highlight the importance of drones in agriculture in Afghanistan, where they can improve agricultural observation, decrease resource waste, and increase crop yields.

Data analytics for well-informed decision-making: clause 14.1.3.

Making sense of massive volumes of agricultural data is impossible without data analytics. In this section, we discuss the value of data analytics, its practical applications, and the difference it makes in making sound judgements. We delve into how data analytics collects, organises, and makes sense of information from a wide variety of sources, empowering farmers to make informed decisions about when and how much to sow, fertilise, and harvest. In addition, we emphasise the role that data analytics may play in raising crop yields by better directing agricultural investments and refining techniques.

Mechanisation: The Might of Machines, 14.2.

Mechanisation, or the use of advanced farm equipment, provides Afghan farmers with a number of benefits, including more productivity and less need for labour. In this article, we'll talk about how important mechanisation is, what kinds of machinery are used, and how that affects farming. We look into the ways in which machinery like tractors and harvesters simplify pre-harvest, harvest, and post-harvest tasks. We also highlight the potential of mechanisation to increase farm output, decrease labour costs, and boost overall efficiency in Afghanistan's farming sector.

Tractors, the backbone of the farming industry, are the subject of Section 14.2.1.

In Afghanistan, tractors serve as multipurpose workhorses that boost agricultural output. In this section, we'll talk about how tractors help with farming and the several ways they can be used. We look at how tractors have helped to mechanise traditionally labor-intensive agricultural operations like planting and ploughing. We also emphasise the potential of tractors to increase output by helping farmers tend to more land with less effort and in less time.

Harvesters' Effectiveness in Collecting Crops (Section 14.2.2)

Reduced post-harvest losses are mostly attributable to the efforts of harvesters. This section delves into the role harvesters play and the effects they have on the process of gathering crops. We take a look at the ways in which harvesters use machinery to speed up and improve the quality of the crucial task of gathering and collecting crops like wheat, rice and maize. We also note how harvesters can help Afghan farmers increase their crop yields by shortening the harvest period and decreasing waste.

Quality Preservation Equipment (Section 14.2.3)

Equipment used after harvest is essential for maintaining crop quality. This section discusses the importance of post-harvest equipment, its various uses, and its effects on preserving crops. We look at how equipment like grain dryers and storage units help to preserve the quality of stored harvests and cut down on losses. We also highlight the role that post-harvest equipment may play in protecting crop quality, extending storage life, and ultimately boosting the economic value of crops for farmers in Afghanistan.

Biotechnology: Realising Agricultural Promise (Section 14.3)

Biotechnology provides novel approaches to boosting crop yields, boosting disease resistance, and adjusting to fluctuating climates. The value of biotechnology, such as GM crops and selective breeding, is discussed here. We look at how biotechnology has led to the development of crops that are more resilient to environmental stresses, provide higher yields, and are pest and disease resistant. The potential of biotechnology to improve agricultural output and food security for farmers in Afghanistan is also highlighted.

Improved yield from genetically modified crops is discussed in Section 14.3.1.

There is hope that genetically modified (GM) crops would greatly increase crop yields. This section discusses the relevance of genetically modified (GM) crops, their distinguishing features, and the effect they have on harvest success. We look at how genetically modified (GM) crops like Bt cotton and herbicide-tolerant soybeans help farmers recover from yield losses caused by pests and weeds. We also emphasise the potential of genetically modified (GM) crops to boost production in Afghan agriculture by making crops more resistant to biotic stressors and enhancing agricultural performance generally.

Tailor-made solutions through precision breeding are discussed in Section 14.3.2.

When it comes to bettering crop types, precision breeding techniques provide individualised answers. The significance of precision breeding, its techniques, and its effects on crop improvement are discussed here. We take a look at how precision breeding helps farmers develop crops with desirable characteristics including resilience to drought, increased nutrient content, and disease resistance. We also highlight the promise of precision breeding in increasing crop yield by equipping Afghan farmers with varieties that thrive in the country's specific climate and satisfy local consumers' preferences.

Digital Answers During the Information Age 14.4

There has been an information revolution in agriculture in Afghanistan thanks to digital solutions such as mobile apps and online platforms. In this article, we discuss the value of digital solutions, some of the ways they might be put to use, and the way they affect people's ability to gain access to information and make sound judgements. We dig into the ways in which farmers can use mobile apps to get information such as weather forecasts, market prices, and pest alarms. We also highlight the potential of digital solutions in promoting a data-driven approach to agriculture in Afghanistan and broadening access to vital information.

Section 14.4.1: Mobile Applications for Easily Accessible Information

Afghan farmers now have easy access to information thanks to mobile apps. This section discusses the value of mobile applications, how they work, and how they affect people's ability to gain access to information. We look into

 how these apps provide useful resources for farmers, such as planting calendars and pest management advice. We also highlight mobile apps' potential to boost crop output in Afghanistan by giving farmers with up-to-the-minute information and individualised suggestions.

Market Intelligence for Online Services (Section 14.4.2)

Afghan farmers benefit greatly from the availability of market information and agricultural statistics on online platforms. In this section, we discuss the value of digital marketplaces, the benefits they offer, and the way they have altered consumers' access to goods and services. We look at how these sites help farmers by giving them access to data on prices, market movements, and trading possibilities. We also highlight the potential of digital marketplaces to increase economic returns in Afghanistan's agricultural sector by facilitating transactions between farmers and consumers.

Balance Sustainability and Environmental Concerns in Section 14.5

Sustainability and environmental concerns must be taken into account as Afghanistan's agricultural sector adopts contemporary technologies to boost output. Here, we look at how sustainable methods can best be applied to today's cutting-edge tools. We look at how sustainable innovation, including resource-saving technologies, ethical applications of biotechnology, and eco-friendly digital approaches, may strike a balance between economic development and environmental protection. We also stress the importance of a sustainable strategy in contemporary agriculture to protect the essential natural resources for agriculture in Afghanistan.

Section 14.5.1: "Resource Efficiency"; "Waste Reduction"

The primary goals of resource-efficient technology are waste minimization and conservation. This section discusses why resource efficiency is important, how it may be put to use, and what kind of waste it can cut down on. The use of controlled-release fertilisers, water-efficient irrigation systems, and precision farming techniques are discussed as means to reduce waste and protect natural resources. We also emphasise the potential of water and soil conservation methods in promoting agriculture's long-term viability in Afghanistan.

Ethical Progress in Responsible Biotechnology, Section 14.5.2

When biotechnology is used ethically, it helps farmers improve their yields without negatively impacting the environment. In this section, we'll discuss the role of ecologically conscious agriculture and the concepts of responsible biotechnology. We look at how biotechnology can be used responsibly in terms of environmental impact, taking into account both immediate and long-term consequences for the environment. We also highlight the role that biotechnology can play in fostering a sustainable middle ground between agricultural development and environmental protection in Afghanistan.

To make educated decisions about digital solutions that are gentler on the environment, see Section 14.5.3.

Digital solutions with a focus on environmental sustainability promote well-informed decision-making. In this section, we discuss the relevance, characteristics, and influence of environmentally friendly digital solutions on environmentally conscious decision-making. We investigate how digital tools might help farmers learn more about greener ways of working and conservation techniques. We also highlight the potential of environmentally aware digital technologies in encouraging environmentally responsible agricultural practises in Afghanistan.

Conclusion

There is no denying that new agricultural technology has the potential to boost output in Afghanistan's farming sector. Precision farming, mechanisation, biotechnology, and digital solutions are potent instruments that provide farmers with insight, facilitate efficiency, and increase harvests. With the help of these innovations, farmers in Afghanistan may improve their standard of living, conserve natural resources, and build a stronger economy.

But it's crucial to check that incorporating these technology follows sound sustainability and environmental management practises. Achieving a balance between technological advancement and ecological preservation can be aided by responsible resource usage, ethical biotechnology applications, and environmentally mindful digital solutions. There is great potential for Afghanistan's agricultural environment to be transformed, farmers' livelihoods to be improved, and the country's agricultural industry to become more resilient and productive as it continues to adopt modern agricultural technologies.

Chapter 9:
Market Exposure Abroad

9.1- Discuss the importance of market access for Afghan agricultural products.

Unlocking Afghanistan's Economic Potential by Expanding Access to Markets for Agricultural Products is discussed in Chapter 15.

Introduction

The economic growth and food security of Afghanistan are directly tied to the country's ability to export agricultural goods. This chapter dives into the transformative significance of market access, analysing its effects on farmers' incomes, food security, and Afghanistan's economic growth. We discuss the possibilities of value addition and diversification, the importance of infrastructure and trade policy, and the obstacles and opportunities associated with expanding the market for Afghan agricultural products both domestically and abroad.

Market Access: A Road to Prosperity, Section 15.1

Farmers in Afghanistan can sell their goods and improve their living conditions if they have easier access to markets. The importance of market access, its many forms, and its effects on farmers' financial security are discussed here. We explore the ways in which farmers' access to markets facilitates the sale of their produce and the resulting income that can be reinvested in their businesses and households. We also highlight the role that access to markets may play in helping farmers in Afghanistan escape poverty and propel the country's economic growth.

Markets Near You, for Urgent Purchases (15.1.1)

Agricultural goods produced in Afghanistan can be sold quickly on local markets. In this part, we examine how local markets help communities meet their economic and nutritional demands as well as their unique qualities. We investigate how farmers might increase food availability and income by selling their wares at local marketplaces where customers live. We also stress the importance of local markets as a way to strengthen food networks, promote economic growth, and increase consumer choice.

Foreign Markets Offer a World of Possibilities, per Section 15.1.2.

The potential for Afghan agricultural exports to international markets is enormous. In this section, we discuss the relevance of global markets, the variety they offer, and the effect they have on fostering growth in commerce and financial gains. We look at how global trade facilitates expansion of the market and the creation of new sources of revenue. We also stress the importance of international markets in helping Afghanistan diversify its agricultural sector, raise incomes, and advance the country's economy.

Market Difficulties and Overcoming Them Section 15.2

While access to markets is essential to economic growth, doing so is not without difficulty. Here, we look at the challenges Afghan farmers and manufacturers have in getting their goods to market, including a lack of value-added production, trade obstacles, and enough infrastructure. We investigate how these obstacles can restrict access to markets and dampen agriculture's economic potential in Afghanistan. We also stress the importance of taking preventative steps and employing strategic approaches to fully realise the economic benefits of expanding access to new markets.

Section 15.2.1: Trade Barriers Caused by Inadequate Infrastructure

Inadequate roads and storage facilities, for example, might be significant barriers to entering the Afghan market. In this part, we discuss the relevance, repercussions, and effect of infrastructure deficits on agricultural commerce. Inadequate transportation and storage facilities are discussed, along with its effects on farmers' access to markets, product quality, and post-harvest losses. We also emphasise the role that better infrastructure may play in expanding farmers' access to markets, raising product quality, and decreasing trade costs in Afghanistan.

Trade Barriers and Managing Overlapping Regulations 15.2.2

Afghan agricultural products may face difficulties breaking into new markets due to trade barriers such as tariffs and sanitary laws. In this section, we will discuss the relevance, consequences, and effect of trade barriers on international trade. We look at how complicated laws and hefty tariffs affect the ability of Afghan farmers to sell their products abroad. We also highlight the possibility of trade policy change and trade facilitation initiatives to remove obstacles to trade for Afghan agricultural goods.

Limited Value Addition: Realising Economic Potential is discussed in Section 15.2.3.

Afghanistan's agricultural exports may be hindered in terms of market access and economic returns due to a lack of value addition in the production process. We explore the relevance of value addition, its advantages, and the effect it has on product quality and market competitiveness in the next section. We investigate how Afghanistan's restricted processing and packaging options limit product variety, shorten product shelf life, and restrict the country's access to international markets. We also emphasise the importance of processing and branding as value-added solutions that can improve product quality and expand the market for Afghan agricultural goods.

Success Strategies for Penetrating New Markets is discussed in Section 15.3.

The agricultural sector of Afghanistan's economy cannot progress without greater access to international markets. Here, we discuss some of the many options available for bringing Afghanistan's agricultural goods to market and realising their full economic potential. Here, we look at how diversification, branding, market data, and international cooperation can improve a company's ability to break into new markets. We also highlight the potential of these measures in promoting economic growth, enhancing food security, and guaranteeing the prosperity of Afghan farmers.

Market resilience can be achieved by diversification (Section 15.3.1).

Farmers can gain market stability through diversification, which opens up their access to a wider variety of

 concerning the marketplace. The importance of diversification, its advantages, and its bearing on market entry are discussed in this section. We look at how farmers in Afghanistan might increase economic security by spreading their crop and product offerings across many markets. We also emphasise the role diversification may play in making the agriculture sector more robust and expanding Afghan goods' availability on international markets.

Branding and Reputation Management (Section 15.3.2)

The branding of Afghan agricultural products is essential to their success in the international market. In this article, we investigate the relevance of branding, its concepts, and the impact it has on product differentiation. We look at how branding helps Afghan products stand out by communicating their superior quality, unique history, and genuineness to consumers. We also draw attention to the role that branding may play in making Afghan agricultural products more competitive in the market, boosting their value, and opening up new sales channels.

Market Data for Well-Informed Choices, Section 15.3.3

In the agricultural industry, having access to market data is crucial for making good judgements. In this section, we discuss the value of market information, where to find it, and how it influences the decisions farmers make. We investigate how knowledge of market conditions—such as price trends, customer preferences, and demand forecasts—helps farmers make better decisions about what to grow and what to sell. We also note the importance of market intelligence in facilitating increased market access in Afghanistan, as it equips farmers there to adapt to shifting market conditions and make decisions that will ultimately increase their income.

Section 15.3.4: Expanding Horizons through International Cooperation

The expansion of market access for Afghan agricultural products is dependent on international cooperation. This section delves into the value of international cooperation, the different ways it might take shape, and the effect it has on commercial ties. Here, we take a look at the ways in which Afghanistan and its neighbours, as well as international development organisations, may work together to increase access to new markets, lower trade obstacles, and create more demand for Afghan exports. We also emphasise the role international cooperation may play in boosting commerce, expanding access to markets, and enhancing the agricultural sector in Afghanistan's economy.

Food safety and economic growth: how market access affects the bottom line

Food security and economic growth in Afghanistan will benefit from increased access to markets for agricultural products produced in the country. Here, we look at how increased access to markets helps maintain a consistent food supply, lowers food costs, and fuels economic expansion. We look at how the availability of markets can help people get better nourishment at a lower cost, and raise people's level of living generally. We also highlight the role that access to markets can play in encouraging domestic production, decreasing trade deficits, and accelerating growth in Afghanistan's economy.

A Reliable Food Supply Is Critical to National Food Security (Section 15.4.1).

A reliable food supply for the populace depends on easy access to markets. In this section, we'll examine the value of a reliable food supply, the advantages it offers, and the role it plays in ensuring enough nutrition. We investigate how increased access to markets ensures a steady supply of food, mitigating shortages and price swings. In addition, we emphasise the role that access to markets can play in ensuring that families in Afghanistan have access to nutritious food, reducing hunger, and enhancing their standard of living.

Reduced Food Prices: Universal Accessibility 15.4.2

Having easier access to the market helps keep food costs down, allowing more people to purchase it. Here, we discuss the importance of lower food prices, their ramifications, and the effect on consumers' ability to spend. We look at how increased access to the market promotes price competition, which in turn gives customers more reasonably priced food choices. We also emphasise the role that access to markets may play in reducing food prices, increasing the availability of healthy food, and boosting the standard of living in Afghanistan.

Economic expansion and its knock-on effects are discussed in Section 15.4.3.

Increasing access to markets boosts economic growth across the board. We explore the relevance, far-reaching effects, and role of economic growth on national development in the next section. We look at how increased access to markets affects several sectors of the economy, from shipping and retail to food processing and packaging, ultimately leading to more jobs and higher wages. We also emphasise the potential of increased market access to aid in Afghanistan's economic development, raise living standards, and decrease poverty.

Conclusion
Agriculture in Afghanistan contributes significantly to the country's GDP, food security, and overall development when it has access to international markets. The ability to sell their goods to both domestic and foreign buyers is crucial to the economic success of farmers. To realise agriculture's full economic potential in Afghanistan, market challenges must be overcome. These include inadequate infrastructure, trade impediments, and low value addition.

Promoting economic growth and development, increasing market access involves diversity, branding, market information access, and international partnership. Farmers, consumers, and the nation as a whole all gain from market access because of its effects on food security, lower food prices, and economic growth.

To ensure a steady food supply, boost economic well-being, and contribute to the nation's overall growth, Afghanistan must continue to improve market access for its agricultural products. The agricultural sector may play a crucial role in Afghanistan's transition to economic independence and growth if it is given better access to markets.

9.2- Analyze the international demand for organic and exotic agricultural products.

Opportunity in the Global Market for Organic and Unique Agricultural Products, Chapter 16

Introduction

Increased interest in healthful eating and culinary adventure have contributed to a meteoric rise in the demand for organic and unusual agricultural goods around the world. Exploring the expansion of organic and exotic markets and the prospects they bring for Afghan agriculture, this chapter looks into the complicated and changing world of international demand for these products. We also discuss the obstacles and solutions Afghan farmers might use to enter this booming international market.

Chapter 16: The Rise of Organic Agriculture Around the World

Organic farming, which relies on conservation techniques and shuns the use of artificial chemicals, is becoming increasingly popular around the world. We discuss the importance of organic agriculture, its guiding principles, and the forces that are increasing the demand for organic goods around the world. We investigate why more people are buying organic food and how rising consciousness about health, the environment, and food safety have contributed to this trend. We also highlight the potential of organic farming to improve farmers' access to markets and earnings in Afghanistan.

Section 16.1.1: The Organic Link to Health and Well-Being

The global demand for organic agricultural goods is mostly driven by the rising interest in health and wellness. In this section, we discuss the relevance of health and wellness, their connections to organic products, and the influence they have on shoppers' purchasing decisions. We investigate the trend of people preferring organic food because of the assumed health benefits it provides. We also note the role that growing interest in organic foods and other wellness-related items may play in expanding sales channels for Afghan farmers.

Concerns about the Environment and Possible Solutions

The demand for organic agricultural products is largely driven by environmental worries, such as climate change and sustainable farming. In this part, we discuss how consumers' concerns for the environment coincide with organic farming and how this influences their purchasing decisions. We look at the reasons why people prefer organic foods and products, such as chemical reduction and biodiversity preservation. We also stress the role environmental consciousness may play in increasing the market for organic goods and spreading the word about the need of eco-friendly farming techniques in Afghanistan.

Subsection 16.1.3: Organic Food and Your Trust in It

The global demand for organic agricultural goods has increased significantly due to worries over food safety. In this section, we discuss the importance of food safety, how it relates to organic goods, and how it affects consumers' faith in the food industry. Here, we investigate why many people believe organic food is preferable because it is healthier for them. Furthermore, we highlight the potential of food safety concerns in boosting demand for organic products and establishing consumer trust in the safety and quality of organic produce in Afghanistan.

Section 16.2: Exploring New Flavours with Unusual Agricultural Ingredients

There is a growing demand around the world for exotic agricultural products due to their distinct tastes, textures, and cultural importance. We discuss the reasons for the high international demand for exotic agricultural goods and the role they play in the global economy. We investigate how people's growing interest in trying out different cuisines, flavours, and ingredients has increased the need for rare and culturally significant agricultural goods. We also highlight exotic agriculture's potential to help diversify Afghanistan's agricultural economy and open up new markets to the country's farmers.

Section 16.2.1: Gastronomic Travel, Regional Flavours

The worldwide interest in trying out different cuisines and trying new flavours has increased the market for unusual agricultural goods. Here, we discuss how the discovery of new foods and ingredients might influence people's preferences for unusual or niche items. We investigate the trend of consumers seeking for unusual ingredients in order to cook dishes with a wide range of flavours and cultural influences. We also note how the interest in trying new foods has the potential to increase the demand for unusual goods, creating new chances for trade for Afghan farmers.

Culture-specific rarity and importance (Section 16.2.2)

The global desire for exotic agricultural crops is heavily influenced by their cultural importance. In this section, we discuss the relevance of cultural value, its connection to unusual goods, and the effect on consumers' tastes. We look at how culturally significant goods like spices, herbs, and traditional ingredients are in great demand because of their place in traditional and authentic cooking. Furthermore, we stress the importance of cultural value in influencing the demand for unusual items and opening up new markets for Afghan agricultural products.

Organic Market Dynamics: Expanding Opportunities, Section 16.3

The market for organically grown food is a growing and exciting industry that might provide a boon to farmers in Afghanistan. The possibilities for Afghan agriculture, as well as the expanding organic market, are discussed below. We investigate the growing interest in organic foods among consumers and the opportunities this presents for producers in Afghanistan. We also stress the significance of international standards and organic certification for entering worldwide organic markets.

Health in Every Bite: Organic Fruits and Vegetables (16.3.1)

Produce grown without the use of harmful pesticides is a major selling point for organic food companies. Here we discuss the importance of organic produce, why people choose to buy it, and how it affects the availability of markets for conventional produce. We dive into the increasing interest in organic versions of commonplace foods like apples, tomatoes, and greens, and how Afghan farmers might benefit from this trend. Furthermore, we stress the importance of organic fruits and vegetables in expanding the market for Afghan farmers and increasing their incomes.

Natural and Nutritious Organic Dairy Products, Section 16.3.2

Natural and nutrient-rich, organic dairy products are in high demand. The importance of organic dairy products, their nutritional content, and their effect on consumer preferences are discussed in this section. We look at the prospects for Afghan farmers to produce high-quality organic dairy and the rising demand for organic milk, cheese, and yoghurt. We also highlight the potential of organic dairy products to increase farm income diversity and meet the rising international demand for organic dairy.

Organic Meat and Poultry: Standards for Quality and Animal Care

Organically raised meat and poultry gives buyers peace of mind about the animals' treatment. We explore the value of organic meat and poultry, their popularity among customers, and their effect on market availability in this section. We look at the growing interest in organic beef, chicken, and lamb and how Afghan farmers might be able to provide this market. We also discuss how organic meat and poultry could help animals, open up new markets, and boost profits for Afghanistan's farmers.

Exotic Market Dynamics: Specialising Markets Section 16.4

The specialist and specialised nature of the exotic agricultural industry presents exceptional prospects for producers in Afghanistan. Here we examine the potential for Afghan agriculture, the dynamics of the exotic market, and the variety of exotic items available. We investigate how Afghan farmers may meet the rising demand for exotic spices, herbs, fruits, and speciality commodities in niche markets. We also stress the significance of meeting all quality, packaging, and international trade standards before entering the world's exotic marketplaces.

Flavorful Signatures of Exotic Spices and Herbs (Section 16.4.1)

The unique flavour and scent of exotic spices and herbs have made them a sought-after component of cuisines around the world. Here, we'll go into the relevance of

 of exotic spices and herbs, their allure to cooks, and the effect on availability on the market. We look at the prospects for Afghan farmers in light of the rising demand for spices like saffron and unique herbs like Afghan basil. We also note the potential of rare spices and herbs to help Afghanistan's agriculture sector break into new markets and boost its economy.

Unique Treasures: Exotic Fruits and Specialty Crops (Section 16.4.2)

Rare and unusual, exotic fruits and speciality crops pique the interest of foodies who value variety and exclusivity. We explore the value of exotic fruits and speciality crops, their appeal, and the effect they have on consumer tastes in the next section. We investigate the opportunities for Afghan farmers to meet the growing demand for pomegranates, figs, and speciality crops like quinoa and saffron. We also emphasise the potential for exotic fruits and specialised crops to open up new markets for Afghan farmers and increase their financial rewards.

Challenges and Strategies for Penetration of International Markets (Section 16.5)

There are obstacles to overcome when trying to break into international markets with organic and unusual agricultural products. Here, we examine some of the challenges that Afghan farmers confront, such as trade rules, market access, organic certification, and quality control. We examine the methods and practises that have proven effective in the face of these difficulties, such as bolstering the value chain, investing in quality, adhering to international standards, and engaging in international trade events. We also highlight the possibilities for cooperation with international organisations and trade partners to help Afghan agricultural products enter worldwide markets.

Organic Certification - Assurance of Quality and Regulations Compliance 16.5.1

The only way for Afghan farmers to gain access to international organic markets is to become certified as organic. In this section, we discuss the value of organic certification, its effect on consumers' confidence, and the opportunities it opens up for businesses. Here, we take a look at what it takes to get organic certification, from meeting standards to ensuring quality. We also emphasise the need of organic certification for gaining customer confidence and breaking into international organic markets for Afghan agricultural goods.

Section 16.5.2: Quality Control - Achieving Global Accreditation

In order to access worldwide markets for organic and exotic crops, Afghan growers must maintain quality control and conform to international standards. In this section, we discuss the value of quality control, how it affects product quality, and how it affects a company's ability to compete in the market. We take a look at how adhering to international standards—from planting to packaging—can benefit Afghan farmers. We also note the importance of quality control in facilitating the export and international competitiveness of Afghan agricultural products.

Market Access & Overcoming Trade Barriers, Section 16.5.3

It is crucial for Afghan farmers to have access to foreign markets and information on how to overcome trade hurdles. The importance of market access, its function in easing international trade, and its bearing on potential exports are discussed in this section. We investigate the ways in which Afghan farmers have adapted to face the difficulties posed by trade barriers such as tariffs, restrictions, and certification. We also emphasise the role that access to markets may play in increasing Afghanistan's ability to sell its agricultural goods and boosting their profile abroad.

International Cooperation: Strengthening Partnerships for Progress Section 16.5.4

Afghanistan's farmers will have much better luck breaking into international markets for organic and unusual agricultural products if they work together with organisations and trade partners from across the world. In this section, we examine the value of international cooperation, how it facilitates trade promotion, and how it contributes to the growth of existing markets. The value of forming strategic alliances with foreign organisations and attending international trade fairs and expositions is investigated. Furthermore, we emphasise the need of international cooperation in facilitating the successful entry of Afghan agricultural products into global markets.

Conclusion

Afghan agriculture has a lot of potential thanks to the growing international market for organic and unusual foods. Farmers in Afghanistan now have access to a larger and more lucrative market because to the rising demand for natural and unusual goods around the world. Afghan farmers can gain access to these profitable markets by learning the factors that are driving this demand, adopting international standards, and taking strategic methods.

Afghanistan is on the cusp of a new era of agricultural trade, connecting with consumers worldwide, promoting sustainable farming practises, and contributing to the economic development and prosperity of the nation as it continues to explore the potential of organic and exotic agricultural products. The potential for Afghan agriculture to take advantage of these shifts in the market is highlighted in this section.

9.3- Explain the process of establishing trade agreements and ensuring product compliance.

Chapter 17: Navigating Global Markets (Establishing Trade Agreements and Ensuring Product Compliance)

Introduction

The worldwide trade of agricultural products relies heavily on the establishment of trade agreements and the maintenance of product compliance. This chapter delves into the intricate and ever-changing procedures necessary to negotiate trade agreements, conform to international product standards, and succeed in the international business arena. We discuss the value of trade agreements, analyse the processes involved in negotiating and enforcing them, and explain why product compliance is so important for entering and being competitive in global markets. We also address the unique difficulties and solutions that face Afghanistan's agricultural sector.

Trade Agreements: The Building Blocks of International Trade

International trade is predicated on trade agreements, which establish the parameters for commercial transactions between countries. The importance of trade agreements, the ways in which they promote international trade, and the circumstances that lead to their emergence are discussed here. We dive into the ways in which trade agreements shape the landscape of international trade, lowering tariffs and other trade obstacles and providing exporters with more stable markets. We also emphasise the importance of trade agreements in facilitating growth, increasing access to markets, and bolstering international collaboration for agricultural exports from Afghanistan.

Bilateral and multilateral agreements span the spectrum of cooperation, as discussed in Section 17.1.1.

Multiple types of trade agreements exist, from those involving only two countries to those involving dozens or hundreds. In this section, we examine bilateral and multilateral agreements, their variety, and the effects on global trade. We discuss how multilateral agreements, like those under the World Trade Organisation (WTO), establish common trade regulations among several countries while bilateral agreements establish specific economic arrangements between two countries. We also note the importance of global and bilateral trade agreements in facilitating the export of agricultural goods from Afghanistan.

Free trade agreements (FTAs) that lower trade barriers are discussed in Section 17.1.2.

Reduced trade barriers, more economic cooperation, and broader market access are all the result of FTAs. The relevance of FTAs, the concepts underlying them, and the effect they have on trade liberalisation are discussed here. We look at how FTAs cut or do away with tariffs, provide trading partners preferential treatment, and lay the groundwork for trade and investment. Furthermore, we highlight the potential of FTAs in expanding access to markets and broadening the range of goods traded by Afghanistan.

World Trade Organisation (WTO) Global Trade Rules Subsection 17.1.3

The World Trade Organisation (WTO) is a supranational body with the authority to regulate and standardise international trade. In this section, we examine the World Trade Organisation (WTO), its function in regulating international trade, and its effect on bilateral and multilateral trade pacts. Our focus is on the World Trade Organisation and its role in facilitating talks, settling trade disputes, and establishing norms for international trade agreements generally and agricultural trade agreements specifically. We also note the

WTO's potential to facilitate open and honest commerce in agricultural goods produced in Afghanistan.

Trade agreement creation is discussed in detail in Section 17.2: The Negotiation Process.

Trade agreements rely heavily on the debates, concessions, and formulation of mutually beneficial terms that take place during the negotiation process. From the outset to the conclusion, the negotiating process and its essential parts are dissected here. How they begin, who participates, and how difficult it is to come to an agreement on trade terms are all topics we investigate. In addition, we stress the importance of skillful negotiating in establishing beneficial trade agreements and expanding access to markets for Afghan agricultural products.

Initiation and Scope - Setting Objectives; Section 17.2.1

Countries first identify their goals and the scope of the agreement during the beginning and scoping phases of trade negotiations. In this section, we discuss the value of initiating a negotiation and determining its scope, as well as their roles in defining trade objectives and their effect on subsequent negotiations. We investigate how countries form their negotiation positions on issues like market access, intellectual property, and technical restrictions. We also emphasise the importance of setting reasonable expectations at the outset of negotiations to help ensure a successful outcome and better trade terms for Afghan agricultural exports.

Trade Rounds and Sessions: Milestones in the Negotiation Process (Section 17.2.2)

Rounds and sessions in trade negotiations are crucial checkpoints along the way. The relevance of trade rounds and sessions, as well as their responsibilities in progressing negotiations and their impact on the growth of trade agreements, are discussed in this section. We take a look at trade rounds, which are meetings where negotiators meet to discuss trade issues, offer ideas, and try to reach an agreement. We also stress the importance of trade rounds and sessions that result in beneficial trade agreements for Afghan agricultural products.

Finding a Middle Ground through Compromise and Alternate Solutions (Section 17.2.3)

Nations typically make concessions and trade-offs in trade discussions in order to find a middle ground. In this section, we discuss the impact of trade-offs and concessions on the bargaining process, as well as their significance in reaching mutually beneficial solutions. We investigate the possibility of countries making sacrifices in exchange for preferential treatment, such as lowering tariffs or accepting regulatory norms. Furthermore, we emphasise the importance of trade-offs and concessions in encouraging cooperation and negotiating fair trade agreements that benefit agricultural goods produced in Afghanistan.

Article 17.3: Guaranteed Conformity to Global Standards

International trade relies heavily on products being compliant with the rules and regulations of the country of import. In this article, we'll discuss the value of product compliance, how it helps facilitate international trade, and what elements play a role in determining the stringency of regulations. Our discussion delves into how meeting international standards for quality, safety, and labelling is crucial for selling in foreign markets. We also highlight the potential of product conformity to improve market access and customer trust for agricultural products produced in Afghanistan.

Quality Standards - Exceeding Expectations is the subject of Section 17.3.1.

Agricultural products must meet quality requirements to be in line with both global legislation and consumer expectations. In this section, we discuss the relevance of quality standards, how they affect product quality, and how they affect market access. We discuss how quality standards are essential for fulfilling international criteria, as they encompass things like product specifications, safety measures, and production methods. We also emphasise the importance of quality standards in facilitating the entry of Afghan agricultural products into foreign markets and assuring their conformity with regulations.

Regulations for Consumer Safety (Section 17.3.2)

Consumers must be protected from potential health and safety dangers linked with agricultural products, which is why safety rules are so important. Here we discuss the importance of safety rules, their function in protecting the public health, and the effect they have on ensuring products are compliant with the law. We look at how safety laws are essential for guaranteeing the safety of agricultural products, and how they cover things like pesticide residues, food additives, and microbiological requirements. We also note the potential for safety rules to help Afghan agricultural products achieve compliance requirements and increase consumer trust.

Labelling must be clear and informative, per the provisions of Section 17.3.3.

Labelling regulations are essential in giving shoppers accurate data about food and farming supplies. The significance of labelling standards, their function in disseminating product information, and their effect on product compliance are discussed in this section. We discuss why it's important for consumers to have access to information about a product's background, components, nutrition facts, and potential allergens through labels. We also emphasise the potential

Impact labelling regulations in fostering consumer knowledge about Afghan agricultural goods and guaranteeing their conformity with regulations.

The Role of Afghan Agriculture in International Trade: Problems and Solutions

Understanding the intricacies of trade agreements and product compliance presents unique difficulties and opportunities for Afghanistan's agricultural sector. Capacity limitations, regulatory harmonisation, and problems gaining access to markets are just a few of the obstacles we examine in this section that Afghan farmers face. Capacity building, regulatory alignment, and market diversification are just some of the methods and best practises we investigate as a means for the agriculture sector in Afghanistan to triumph over these obstacles. We also highlight the possibilities of regional integration and international cooperation to aid Afghan agriculture in international trade.

Subsection 17.4.1: Enhancing Capabilities by Developing New Abilities

To better understand and implement the requirements of international standards and trade agreements, capacity training is essential for Afghan farmers. To further understand the relevance of capacity building, its role in enhancing the capacities of Afghan farmers, and its effect on product conformity and trade negotiations, we will go into each of these topics in the following subsections. We discuss how training programmes, technical aid, and knowledge transfer all play a role in capacity building to help Afghan farmers face the obstacles of international trade. The potential of capacity building to strengthen Afghan agriculture and increase its competitiveness on global markets is also highlighted.

Section 17.4.2: Regulatory Harmonisation, or Compliance with Abroad

In order for Afghan agriculture to conform to international standards and satisfy product requirements, regulatory alignment is crucial. The relevance of regulatory alignment, its function in bringing Afghan legislation into line with international norms, and its effect on product compliance are all discussed in this section. We look at how bringing laws and institutions into line with international standards requires changes to both. We further emphasise the possibility of regulatory congruence in guaranteeing product compliance and easing market access for agricultural products from Afghanistan.

Section 17.4.3: Expanding Market Opportunities

To lessen its reliance on one market and broaden its potential trade partners, Afghan agriculture might diversify its market. This section delves into the importance of market diversification, how it can help increase market access, and how it can strengthen trade resilience. We look at how expanding farmers' access to diverse trading partners and new markets can help mitigate trade risks for Afghanistan. Further, we stress the need of market diversity in protecting Afghan agriculture from price swings and expanding access to new markets.

International Cooperation and the Promotion of Commercial Links Section 17.5

When it comes to international trade, Afghan agriculture relies heavily on international cooperation and engagement with trade partners and organisations. Here we look at how international collaboration affects trade agreements and product conformity, as well as its significance and role in building trade ties. We investigate how international collaboration might help the agricultural sector in Afghanistan by forming partnerships with nearby nations, international organisations, and trade development agencies. We also stress the importance of international cooperation to increase the visibility of Afghan agricultural products on international markets and boost the country's economy.

Conclusion

For Afghan agriculture to succeed in global markets, it is crucial to first establish trade agreements and then ensure product compliance. Facilitating economic development and expanding access to markets for Afghan agricultural products, trade agreements are negotiated on a bilateral, multilateral, and within the framework of international organisations like the World Trade Organisation.

Agricultural products from Afghanistan that are exported to other countries must comply with international regulations concerning quality standards, food safety, and labelling in order to ensure that they are up to par with what buyers abroad expect. Farmers in Afghanistan can help their country flourish and develop if they are helped to negotiate the complexities of international trade, gain access to a wide variety of international markets, and work together with their counterparts around the world. This section highlights the opportunities for Afghan agriculture to prosper in international trade if certain guidelines and tactics are adopted.

Chapter 10:
Stories of Achievement and Case Studies

10.1- Share real-life case studies of Afghan farmers and entrepreneurs who have successfully unlocked their agricultural export potential.

Afghan Agricultural Entrepreneurs Succeed in International Markets, Chapter 18: Real-World Examples

Introduction

Afghan farmers and businesspeople who have unlocked the country's agricultural export potential are inspiring examples of the power of hard work, creativity, and perseverance. In this chapter, we provide real-world case studies of individuals and businesses that have successfully navigated international markets by adapting to new environments, capitalising on opportunities, and making considerable progress. These examples not only serve as sources of motivation, but also as lessons in the tactics and methods that can propel Afghan agriculture to new heights on the international scene.

Saffron's Success: The Rise of a Prosperous Industry

Afghan farmers and businesspeople have found success exporting saffron, also called "red gold," to international markets. Here, we look into the saffron industry's success tales, discussing how Afghan saffron has become renowned around the world. In this article, we take a closer look at the saffron boom and the farmers who shifted from poppy production to this lucrative industry, as well as the cooperatives that have played an important role in ensuring equitable pricing and quality assurance.

Wahid's Saffron Cooperative, Case Study 18.1.1

Wahid, a farmer in the province of Herat, recognised the value of saffron and decided to join a cooperative. Wahid gained knowledge about contemporary saffron cultivation practises and quality assurance tests through the cooperative. He was able to start exporting saffron to places like India and the United Arab Emirates with the help of the cooperative. Wahid's success has improved his financial situation and encouraged other farmers to start growing saffron, which has improved their lot in life and boosted the local economy.

Maryam's Saffron is the subject of Case Study 18.1.2.

Maryam, a businesswoman in Kabul, recognised an opening in exporting branded Afghan saffron. She set up a factory to process and package saffron and launched a brand that highlighted the product's exceptional quality and Afghani heritage. Maryam's saffron became well-known in markets all over the world, including Europe and the United States, because to her commitment to quality and marketing. Her achievement exemplifies the power of value addition and branding in breaking into foreign markets.

Pomegranate Success: From Fields to Foreign Markets (Section 18.2)

Thanks to the efforts of producers and exporters who saw the global demand for this nutritious fruit, pomegranates, a popular fruit in Afghanistan, have become an important export item. Here, we delve into pomegranate success tales, illuminating how Afghan pomegranates have made it to foreign markets thanks to their high quality and delicious flavour.

Naser's Pomegranate Orchard: A Case Study 18.2.1

Naser, a farmer from Kandahar, decided to take on the challenge of modernising and exporting his pomegranate crop. Naser enhanced the management, pest control, and post-harvest processing of his orchard with the help of training programmes and assistance from the Ministry of Agriculture, Irrigation, and Livestock (MAIL). So, his pomegranates may be sent to places like Pakistan and India, where quality is very important. The potential for Afghan pomegranates in worldwide markets is demonstrated by Naser's success, and by extension, the impact of agricultural extension programmes.

Sara's Export Company: Case Study 18.2.2

Sara, an enterprising young woman, set out to create a business to export Afghan pomegranates. Sara specialised in pomegranates that were grown organically and naturally since she saw a growing demand for such products around the world. She collaborated closely with Afghan farmers to help them gain access to markets outside of their country. She attributes the company's success to its dedication to ethical sourcing and environmentally responsible procedures. Sara's business now exports Afghan pomegranates all the way to Europe, the Middle East, and beyond.

Section 18.3: The Raisin Renaissance: Commercialising an Old Way of Life

For decades, raisins have been an integral part of Afghan cuisine. However, it took forward-thinking farmers and businesspeople to turn this staple into a profitable export. Here, we delve into the sultana comeback tales, explaining how Afghan raisins became a sought-after commodity on store shelves around the world.

Ahmad's Solar Drying Project (Case Study 18.3.1)

Ahmad, a farmer in Balkh province, saw a market opportunity in the worldwide demand for premium raisins. He launched a solar drying venture to compete in this sector. Ahmad embraced cutting-edge drying practises and set up a solar drying plant with the help of a community-based agricultural development programme. His carefully tended raisins, dried to perfection, eventually made it to stores across Europe and North America. The success of Ahmad's exports highlights the significance of innovation and enhanced post-harvest practises.

The Raisin Cooperative of Farida, Case 18.3.2

A proactive businesswoman, Farida founded a sultana cooperative in Herat with the goal of uniting local farmers in order to increase sultana quality and open up international markets. The cooperative helped farmers learn about best practises for growing, inspecting, and selling raisins. Afghan raisins are exported to nations like India and Russia thanks to the cooperative's efforts to acquire contracts on a global scale. The cooperative model implemented in Farida demonstrates the power of working together to increase access to markets for Afghan agricultural goods.

A Success Story (Section 18.4): Bringing Nuts to the World Market

Almonds and pistachios grown in Afghanistan are often regarded as some of the best in the world. In this article, we examine the nut industry's rise to international prominence and the role it plays in boosting Afghanistan's economy and providing revenue to the country's farmers.

Almond Orchard in Abdul's Case Study 18.4.1

A Nangarhar farmer named Abdul saw the potential for Afghan almonds on international markets. Using resources from a horticulture improvement project, he upgraded his almond orchard to one that employs cutting-edge techniques like grafting and pest management. Abdul's almonds were highly sought after in international markets including India and the Middle East due to their exceptional quality and flavour. The significance of modernization and the potential of Afghan nuts in worldwide trade are highlighted by his accomplishments.

Success Strategies and Overcoming Adversity in Section 18.5

In spite of the difficulties they've faced, Afghan farmers and business owners have achieved remarkable success. Access to capital, quality control, entering new markets, and overcoming trade restrictions are just some of the issues we examine in this part as they are shared by the individuals and businesses included in the case studies. We also identify critical strategies and best practises, like capacity building, value creation, and innovation, that contributed significantly to their success.

strategy, coordinated efforts, and brand integration.

Access to Financial Resources - An Engine for Economic Development

When trying to expand their agricultural exports, many Afghan farmers and business owners struggle to gain access to necessary funding. In this section, we'll look at the ways in which the case study participants raised money, including through grants, private investments, and agricultural development programmes. This shows how crucial financial aid is to the development and improvement of agriculture in Afghanistan.

Quality Assurance Procedures That Effortlessly Accommodate Global Standards Subsection 18.5.2

For Afghan agricultural products to reach international standards, it is essential that quality control be maintained. Individuals and businesses are shown in the case studies to have invested in training, cutting-edge methods, and quality control in order to manufacture goods that can compete on a global scale. The takeaway here is that strict QC practises can boost product viability and allow access to new foreign markets.

Section 18.5.3: Expanding Market Opportunities

The case studies all share the difficulty of breaking into new markets, and the solutions range from attending trade shows to forming global alliances. These methods demonstrate how taking preventative steps, such as diversifying and collaborating internationally, to boost market access can result in more chances to export goods and services.

Trade Barriers and Overcoming Difficulties, Section 18.5.4

The case studies show that trade obstacles are a significant problem for agricultural exporters in Afghanistan. Regulatory alignment, teamwork, and innovation are some of the methods utilised to overcome these challenges. The ability to persevere and adjust to new circumstances is highlighted by these examples of achievement.

Future Hope - Expanding on Past Achievements Section 18.6

The success stories of actual Afghan farmers and business owners in the global market give us reason to be optimistic about the future of agriculture in Afghanistan. Afghanistan's agricultural export potential can be boosted by the methods, innovations, and collaborative approaches demonstrated by these individuals and organisations. Afghan agriculture has a bright future ahead of it if it can capitalise on its recent triumphs and overcome its current obstacles.

Conclusion

Afghan farmers and business owners' achievements speak volumes about the market potential of Afghan agriculture. Individually, these people have changed their lives and contributed greatly to

Afghanistan's economic growth through their embrace of innovation, quality improvement, and market diversity. Their experiences demonstrate the vast potential for agricultural export that exists in Afghanistan, and they act as inspirations to the country's whole agricultural community. This section serves as a tribute to their efforts and an impetus for further development of Afghan agriculture on the global scale.

10.2- Highlight the impact of these success stories on rural communities and the national economy.

Harvesting Success: Chapter 19's Effect on Rural Areas and the Economy as a Whole

Introduction

The achievements of Afghan farmers and businesspeople who have realised their full potential in the agricultural export market go much beyond any single success story. These triumphs have far-reaching effects on rural areas and the Afghan economy as a whole, fostering development, bettering people's standard of living, and increasing the country's standard of living. This chapter delves into the far-reaching effects of these success stories, examining how they have improved rural residents' quality of life and boosted the country's economy.

Transforming Rural Life: Boosting Livelihoods is discussed in Section 19.1.

Individual and family livelihoods in rural Afghanistan have been revolutionised thanks to the achievements of farmers and businesspeople in the country. In this article, we take a closer look at how improved economic security and quality of life have come to rural communities as a result of greater access to export markets and higher income from agriculture. We look at how increased agricultural income has translated into concrete benefits in the areas of education, healthcare, and housing.

Opportunities for Further Study, Section 19.1.1

Better educational options have become available to rural youngsters as a result of higher agricultural incomes. Families are now better able to provide for their children's education by paying for preschool, elementary, middle, and high school, as well as college. With a better foundation laid for the next generation, rural areas can begin to experience sustainable growth.

Section 19.1.2: Expanded Access to Healthcare

As a result of increased agricultural income, rural populations have seen an uptick in their access to healthcare services. Health outcomes and general prosperity have increased as a result of increased access to affordable medical care for families. The success stories have improved the quality of life for rural residents in more ways than one.

Improved Infrastructure and Living Conditions (Section 19.1.3)

As a result of the success stories, rural residents have been able to put money towards improvements to their homes and communities. Many have been able to construct new houses or improve existing ones, raising their family in safer environments. The standard of living in rural areas can be raised by the improvement of housing and infrastructure.

Employment Opportunities Create a Domino Effect (Section 19.2)

Employment options outside of farming are created as a direct result of agricultural success stories, which in turn has a direct impact on rural communities. The expansion of the agricultural export sector has spawned a number of ancillary companies, including those responsible for processing, packaging, transporting, and marketing agricultural products. Youth and women in rural areas have benefited from this growing employment sector.

Employment in the Processing and Packaging Sector (Section 19.2.1)

More facilities to process and package agricultural products have opened as a result of the success stories. Consequently, this has resulted in increased need for workers in the agricultural product sorting, cleaning, and packing industries. Many people from rural areas have found work in the processing and distribution phases of the supply chain.

Transportation and logistics are discussed in Section 19.2.2.

The importance of transportation and logistics in agricultural exports has grown in recent years. Demand for transportation services has been boosted by these success stories, leading to an increase in rural employment for drivers, labourers, and logistics specialists.

Sales and Promotion (Section 19.2.3)

Marketing and sales positions have been created as a result of the success stories. Many rural entrepreneurs and young people are now working in fields that involve the domestic and worldwide promotion of agricultural products. Export opportunities and market penetration both benefit greatly from these roles.

A Catalyst for Change: Section 19.3's Focus on Women and Young People

The agricultural success stories have had an especially positive effect on rural women and young people. Here, we explore the ways in which women and young people have made significant contributions to the agricultural export sector, thereby fostering economic growth and promoting gender parity.

Agriculture; women's roles; [Section 19.3.1]

The examples of success have created new opportunities for women to work in agriculture. Saffron, pomegranate, and nut and dried fruit farming have all shown an increase in female participation. This improves not only their financial situation, but also their ability to affect change in their communities.

Subsection 19.3.2: Young People and Business.

The success tales have encouraged and inspired young people in rural areas to consider agricultural business. There has been a rise in the number of young people working in organic farming, agribusiness, and value addition. Their participation not only helps to preserve agricultural customs but also revitalises the industry with new perspectives and methods.

Section 19.4: Input to the National Economy, a Key Factor

Agriculture's success stories have revitalised rural areas and become a major contributor to Afghanistan's economy. We examine the role of agricultural exports in the expansion of the economy, the maintenance of a positive trade balance, and the maintenance of adequate food supplies.

Economic Expansion (Section 19.4.1)

The success stories have been significant in boosting the Afghan economy. New revenue streams have been established, increasing the nation's Gross Domestic Product (GDP), thanks to the increased export of agricultural products. The positive effects of this economic expansion trickle down to many different fields.

Section 19.4.2: Enhancement of Trade Balance

The agricultural success stories have helped Afghanistan's trade balance immensely. The trade imbalance has shrunk as a result of the country's increased earnings from exporting agricultural products.

This has strengthened the economy's foundation, making it more resistant to external shocks.

Subsection 19.4.3: Boosting Food Safety

Because to the success of the agricultural export sector, Afghanistan now has a more secure food supply. The country has lessened its reliance on food imports thanks to its agricultural diversification, which has prioritised the cultivation and export of high-value commodities including saffron, pomegranates, almonds, and dried fruits. As a result, there is now more food security and less risk of being affected by changes in global food prices.

Challenges and Future Strategies: What We've Learned

Afghan agriculture's success stories are an inspiration, but they aren't without their own difficulties. Here, we dissect some of the more ubiquitous obstacles mentioned in the success stories, including lack of resources, poor quality control, difficulty breaking into new markets, and hurdles to international trade. Capacity building, value addition, branding, and cooperative approaches are just some of the important tactics and best practises we glean from their successes.

Access to Financial Resources, a Critical Facilitator (19.5.1)

In all the success tales, getting money has been a problem, but the solutions have all been different. The achievements demonstrate the significance of financial support in promoting development and creativity in Afghan agriculture.

Subsection 19.5.2: Quality Control: Gaining a Business Advantage.

It has been crucial to uphold quality control in order for agricultural products to conform to international norms. Increasing product competitiveness and gaining access to new foreign markets are both discussed, along with the need of adhering to quality control procedures, as shown by the case studies.

Market Access: A Route to Development, Section 19.5.3

Participating in trade shows and forming international relationships are only two of the many methods used to overcome the common obstacle of breaking into new markets highlighted by the success tales. These methods demonstrate how taking preventative steps, such as diversifying and collaborating internationally, to boost market access can result in more chances to export goods and services.

To overcome trade barriers, see "Subsection 19.5.4."

The success stories emphasise the fact that trade obstacles are a typical challenge encountered by Afghan agricultural exporters. Regulatory alignment, teamwork, and innovation are some of the methods utilised to overcome these challenges. The ability to persevere and adjust to new circumstances is highlighted by these examples of achievement.

Section

19.6: Bright Prospects - Continuing Success

The positive examples show how Afghan agriculture may contribute to rural economies and the national economy. Afghan agriculture has a bright future full of opportunities for growth, wealth, and sustainable development if its leaders learn from the past and act on the lessons they've gained through overcoming obstacles.

Conclusion

Afghanistan's rural communities and national economy have benefited greatly from the success stories of farmers and entrepreneurs who have unlocked the country's agricultural export potential. These accounts shine as rays of light, revealing the enormous difference that a few motivated people can make in the world. They have not only received the fruits of success but planted the seeds for a bright future in Afghan agriculture through their resiliency, creativity, and cooperation. This section serves as both a tribute to their accomplishments and a rallying cry for the Afghan agricultural community to continue building on their recent momentum.

10.3- Conclude the book with a reflection on the future prospects of Afghanistan's agricultural sector.

Finally, Reaping the Benefits of Sowing the Seeds of Future Success

As we wrap off this in-depth look at Afghanistan's potential for exporting agricultural goods, we turn our attention to the future, where the prospects for Afghanistan's agricultural sector hold the promise of transformation, progress, and prosperity. In the preceding chapters, we have begun to unravel the complex tapestry that is Afghanistan's agricultural history, including its struggles and tribulations, its obstacles, and the amazing success stories that have emerged despite them. As we look back on our journey, we can't help but think about the exciting new era of agricultural innovation that is about to begin in Afghanistan.

First, we'll look at the bright side of things: Afghanistan's agricultural potential.

With its strong base in centuries of agricultural traditions and the potential for growth and development, Afghanistan's agricultural sector has an optimistic future. Opportunities for grain production and animal management span a wide spectrum thanks to Afghanistan's varied agro-ecological zones, which range from the lush plains of Kunduz to the high-altitude terraces of Bamyan. There is a lot of unutilized land, water, and labour that may be put to good use in the agricultural industry.

Section 2: "Ag History Lessons: Afghanistan's Enduring Farmland"

The agricultural sector in Afghanistan has shown extraordinary endurance throughout its history, despite facing several threats from war, political unrest, and natural disasters. The agricultural community draws strength and insight from the lessons of the past.

Farmers have shown resilience and creativity by continually adjusting their methods to fit the evolving landscape.

Part Three: Conquering Difficulties and Charting a Future

The agriculture industry of Afghanistan is confronting a number of difficulties, but they are not insurmountable. Insightful responses and coordinated efforts, as we've seen in prior chapters, can help lessen the severity of these difficulties. Targeted investment, policy reforms, and community engagement can solve the problems of inadequate infrastructure, water supply, and safety. These difficulties can be turned into advantages with the cooperation of the public and commercial sectors.

Section 3.1: Infrastructure Construction

As was mentioned in earlier chapters, the construction of transport and storage facilities is crucial to the agricultural sector's evolution. Post-harvest losses may be minimised, new markets can be reached, and the competitiveness of Afghan agricultural products can be boosted with the help of investments in road networks, cold storage facilities, and sophisticated packaging centres.

Water Management, Section 3.2

Success in agriculture in the future hinges on efficient water management, a topic that has come up often in our examination. Smart water management, including the use of modern irrigation methods and the implementation of water-saving practises, can alleviate water scarcity and guarantee a steady supply of water for agricultural purposes.

Adaptation to Climate Change (Section 3.3)

The problem of how agriculture will be affected by climate change is one that is still developing, and will require innovative solutions. Afghan farmers can adjust to the new weather patterns by increasing their use of drought-resistant crop varieties, adopting environmentally friendly farming methods, and growing a wider variety of crops. Afghanistan can secure its agricultural future by funding climate-resilient agriculture.

The Fourth Section: Knowledge and Technology as a Growth Accelerator

Knowledge and technology are important to the development of Afghanistan's agriculture economy. The use of modern farming techniques, technology, and technological aids has the potential to increase yields while decreasing post-harvest waste. Providing farmers with the education and extension services that disseminate information and technical know-how is essential if they are to adapt to the ever-changing agricultural world.

Agricultural Education and Extension Services, as outlined in Section 4.1.

Improving Afghan farmers' knowledge and abilities is mostly dependent on agricultural education and extension services. Afghanistan can keep its agricultural workers competitive and up-to-date on best practises, crop management, and pest control if it invests in these services. Even the most distant farmers can benefit from agricultural extension, which can be brought to them no matter where they live.

Subsection 4.2: State-of-the-Art Farming Equipment

Precision farming, agroforestry, and mechanisation are only a few examples of the cutting-edge agricultural technology that should be implemented to maximise output while minimising waste. These innovations have the potential to raise agricultural productivity, increase the efficiency of land use, and lessen the negative effects of farming on the environment. They are essential to the long-term success of farming in Afghanistan.

Market Access: A Gateway to Global Prosperity

Agriculture in Afghanistan has a lot of potential in the global market. Afghanistan must prioritise trade agreements, product compliance, and market access if it is to realise its full potential. A thriving agricultural economy in Afghanistan will require the development of trade agreements, the upkeep of quality standards, and the cultivation of worldwide demand.

Section 5.1: International Partnerships and Trade Agreements

Gaining entry to new markets is facilitated by negotiating trade deals with nearby states and international allies. By fostering economic connections, Afghanistan may take advantage of its position as a land bridge between Central and South Asia, allowing for the easier export of agricultural products. Afghanistan can increase its influence in international trade by taking part in talks and securing favourable terms.

Section 5.2: Product Quality and Compliance

Accessing foreign markets requires products that conform to international norms. By following quality standards, safety laws, and labelling requirements, Afghanistan can boost its reputation as a producer of high-quality agricultural goods. Afghan exports can win the trust of buyers around the world if they adhere to strict quality standards.

International Interest in Afghan Goods (Section 5.3)

The growing interest in organic and unusual products around the world has increased the market for Afghanistan's agricultural exports. Saffron, pomegranates, almonds, and dried fruits are just some of Afghanistan's specialties that might help the country cash in on this trend. Afghanistan can ensure its economic future by adapting its manufacturing sector to global trends and expanding its product range.

value in the international economy.

Chapter 6, The Inspirational Role in Success

Afghans might find hope in the documented success stories of farmers and business owners given in earlier chapters. These pioneers have planted the seeds of hope for others to follow in their footsteps by unlocking the potential of agricultural exports. Their experiences have taught them that perseverance, creativity, and teamwork are crucial to achieving success.

Access to Financial Resources, a Critical Facilitator

Afghanistan's agricultural achievements would not have been possible without ready access to credit. Growth and new ideas have been propelled by the accessibility of funds through public initiatives, agricultural improvement programmes, and private sector investments. Evidence of success highlights the value of investment in the agriculture industry.

Subsection 6.2: Quality Assurance and Guaranteed Success

Agricultural success in Afghanistan can be directly attributed to strict quality control measures. These examples show how following quality control procedures can increase product competitiveness and open doors to foreign markets.

Access to Markets: Opportunities for Expansion (Section 6.3)

All the success stories have one thing in common: they all struggled to break into new markets. To overcome this obstacle, the companies involved tried everything from attending trade shows to forming international collaborations. These methods show how diversification and international cooperation, two proactive tactics to improve market access, can result in more chances to export goods and services.

Trade Barriers and Overcoming Obstacles (Section 6.4)

Success stories show trade constraints as a persistent difficulty for agricultural exporters in Afghanistan. Regulatory alignment, teamwork, and innovation are some of the methods utilised to overcome these challenges. The ability to persevere and adjust to new circumstances is highlighted by these examples of achievement.

Subsection 7: Keeping the Good Times Rolling and Moving Forward

As we wrap off this extensive examination, we are left with an uplifting message of possibility and perseverance. Afghanistan's agriculture sector will continue to thrive in the future thanks to the country's pioneering mindset, unwavering dedication, and widespread willingness to work together. To maintain the gains made in removing barriers to agriculture export potential, we need a concerted effort from across all sectors of society and economy.

Subsection 7.1: Working Together and Forming Alliances

The future of agriculture depends on cooperation and teamwork. To further the interests of the sector, the government, the corporate sector, non-governmental organisations, and international partners must all work together. All of these parties can work together to improve conditions for development, investment, and expansion.

Section 7.2: Investment and Policy Changes

The future of agriculture in Afghanistan depends on comprehensive policy reforms and strategic investment. Government efforts should be directed towards implementing policies that encourage development, reward farmers, and lower trade obstacles. The future of the industry can only be secured by investing in its physical infrastructure, technological advancements, and people resources.

Subsection 7.3: Youth and Female Empowerment

There is a moral and financial responsibility to increase the participation of women and young people in agriculture. By opening doors for these populations, Afghanistan can tap into a wealth of unrealized potential. Improve the agricultural industry's prospects by investing in programmes and initiatives that empower women and young people to work in agriculture.

Stewardship of the Environment, per Section 7.4

Protecting the environment is crucial to the long-term success of the agricultural sector in Afghanistan. To ensure the industry's long-term viability, soil conservation, water management, and environmental protection practises must be implemented. Afghanistan can protect its natural resources for future generations if it adopts eco-friendly agriculture practises.

Section 8: The Future of Afghan Agriculture Is Bright

As we wrap out this in-depth investigation, we do so with hope and excitement for what the future holds. The optimistic outlook for Afghanistan's agriculture industry reflects the country's strength, resolve, and potential for revitalization. Afghan agriculture can play a crucial role in the country's economic development and stability with the correct combination of strategic planning, policy reforms, investment, and innovation.

Afghanistan's agricultural export potential is still being unlocked after years of hard work, some major successes, and the country's resilient people. This is an adventure that draws on the knowledge of the past, the experience of the present, and the hope of the future for its direction. We move forward with the knowledge that agriculture in Afghanistan has the potential to become a thriving and profitable pillar of the country's economy.

We hope this extensive evaluation has given you new ideas and a sense of direction for moving forward. The examples of achievement, difficulties, and solutions detailed here are more than just recollections of the past; they are guides to a more promising future. Afghanistan's agricultural sector, population, and land may all expect to flourish in the future if the country's fertile soil is cared for properly today.

The path may be long and the obstacles formidable, but Afghanistan's agriculture industry can reach its full potential with persistence, creativity, and teamwork. The hope for a prosperous and secure agricultural future is not far off; it just needs some TLC and acceptance. As the country enters the international marketplace, it bears the hardiness of its farmers, the knowledge of its history, and the hope for a prosperous future.

Let us, then, set out on this adventure with the conviction that the prospects for agriculture in Afghanistan are an inspiration, a story of perseverance, and a tribute to the unyielding will of a people who live in a land that has always been and always will be the nexus of hope and possibilities. The globe eagerly anticipates the fruits of Afghanistan's agricultural development in the future.